THE MONEY TREE MYTH

A Parents' Guide to Helping Kids Unravel the Mysteries of Money

GAIL VAZ-OXLADE

Stoddart

Published in 1996 by
Stoddart Publishing Co. Limited
34 Lesmill Road
Toronto, Canada
M3B 2T6
Tel (416) 445-3333
Fax (416) 445-5967

Stoddart Books are available for bulk purchase for sales promotions,
premiums, fundraising, and seminars. For details, contact the
Special Sales Department at the above address.

ISBN 0-7737-5817-8

Canadian Cataloguing in Publication Data
is available from the National Library of Canada.

Cover Design: Bill Douglas at The Bang
Printed and bound in Canada

*Stoddart Publishing gratefully acknowledges the support
of the Canada Council, and the Ontario Arts Council,
in the development of writing and
publishing in Canada.*

CONTENTS

5 MAKING MONEY   62

6 DEVELOPING A SPENDING PLAN   83

7 KEEPING MONEY   97

Thanks Y'All

Thanks to all those who took time to review the manuscript and provide me with their wonderful insights. Thanks in particular to Pat Boyle, who squeezed in a draft while on vacation, and to her daughter, Nora, who also pitched in!

To Mom and Dad, who started me off on the right foot and bugged the hell out of me every time it looked as if I might be going astray.

And, once again, thanks to my husband, Kenny, on whom I rely for his soft honesty and enduring patience.

Gail E.

My darling Alexandra,

I dedicate this to you and thank you for being so patient and kind. I hope you will always be my willing teacher.

I love you biggest!

Mommy

INTRODUCTION

When I was about 12, my dad challenged me to get into the savings habit. He told me that for every dollar I saved from my pocket money — I got two dollars a week in allowance — he would match my savings and we would open up my first bank account. We set a deadline for the end of the year and he left it at that.

I guess my dad really knew me well. No more needed to be said. I quickly recognized the value of doubling my money and off I set to save as much as I could by our target date. I had an empty magnum champagne bottle our next-door neighbor had given me. I don't think Mrs. Drew had any idea that her present was going to set me off on a career path even I couldn't have imagined. Each time I had extra money, I pushed it into the bottle. While the bottle was a dark green, I could still see the bills accumulating at the bottom, and the thrill of wondering how much I was going to make my dad shell out kept me going.

Money isn't something most parents talk about with their kids. Unfortunately, like sex, marriage and raising children, money is thought to be one of those things that either you do well or you don't. There are no pre-university courses that talk about how to save, invest and manage your money. That's a pretty big hole in our schools' curriculum. But then again, no one seems interested in preparing children for most of life's mysteries.

Some things are best handled at home. Not! Everything is best handled in a variety of environments. Life is a variety of places, people and things. Without a big-picture approach to teaching our children, we instil in them the idea that everything needs to be compartmentalized.

I see it all the time in dealing with people who are searching for answers to their money questions. Our money is put into a variety of boxes — how much we make, how much we spend, how much we owe, how much we have left. But the fact is, money is money. Only by bringing it all together can we ever really get a handle on how to make it work for us.

There are lots of reasons we don't talk to our children about money. For most of us, money was never a topic for discussion at home. And since attitudes towards money change, the messages we get from our parents, from society and from those "in the know" also keep changing.

Is money dirty? It's probably no dirtier than the sandbox at the local playground, but we have no problem letting our children roll in that stuff. Does money breed greed? Greed is something that manifests itself in all sorts of ways — children get greedy long before they know what money is, so money itself isn't really the culprit. Is money the root of all evil? I doubt that most of the true evil in this world is motivated by money.

Money is something we have to teach our children to live with. They need to know how it works and how to use it. And they need to know just where it fits in life's priorities. But you can't teach a child to ride a bicycle without first covering the concept of balance. And balance, as in every other aspect of our lives, is the key.

There is an old saying I'd like to put my own spin on:

Educate a man, you educate a person.
Educate a woman, you educate a family.
Educate a child and you educate the future.

So this book is all about teaching children about money. It's about some of the fun you can have with money, lessons in value and how to balance what you *need* with what you *want*. It's putting the appropriate amount of emphasis, effort and education on a tool that can be used to meet our basic needs and make dreams come true.

The material in this book is designed to lead children, from the age of about three onwards, through the information they will need to put money into perspective and learn to use it to their advantage. There are several Fun with Money exercises, as well as Money Lessons, designed to help you give your kids the practical experiences they will need to incorporate these ideas into their own reality. These exercises and lessons have been age-banded to give you an idea of the age appropriateness of the activity for your child. But as I'm apt to say over and over, you are the best judge of what is appropriate for your child, and I leave the final decision about what to teach when up to you.

As the book progresses, you will see that it becomes more complex and involved. In some instances I suggest, if your child is old enough and motivated, that you assign the reading and then discuss the information presented. Some parents may even find that the more sophisticated money concepts are new to them. In that case, you and your children can share the learning experience.

I believe very strongly that a focus on learning how to handle our finances, started at an early age, will help to prepare our children to be sound money managers and happier — because they are in control — adults. Some people believe that concepts such as working for money, budgeting and charging interest on a loan extended to a child are PREMATURE . . . WRONG . . . MEAN. Strong reactions such as these demonstrate just how different people can feel about a topic as "simple" as money. Let's face it, there is no great philosophical debate raging about the inherent goodness or badness of money. Most of us recognize that it's a part of life — that it's a tool and we need to figure out how it works to make it work for us. ***But if you believe, as I do, that it is a parent's responsibility to teach his or her children so they can practise in safety, fail where the consequences aren't life changing, and grow confident under the guidance of those who love and care for them most, then this book is for you!***

My daughter, Alexandra, started to show an interest in money when she was 18 months old. She had already discovered it was important; after all, it was everywhere. It could be found in Nanny's purse, in Mommy's wallet and falling from Daddy's pants when he took them off and threw them over the chair. She liked to collect the change in the house and put it in her piggy bank. In fact, she'd go to great extremes to get at the household change pot in order to fill her own coffers. She didn't understand what money was. She knew it was shiny. She knew it made a neat sound as it clattered against the other change she'd collected. It wasn't dirty and there wasn't anything inherently wrong with it.

How we deal with money in our household will have a tremendous impact on the value Alex will eventually place on the stuff. My husband and I have very different attitudes towards money. Between us, we will create a balance for Alex. And what we actually do with our money will have a significant impact on how she sees the way money should fit into her life.

It's amazing how much time we spend telling our children why they can't have money. "Mommy doesn't have any money with her now." "You can't have everything you want." "Do you think money grows on trees?" Yet we spend so little time actually teaching our children how to use money and how the various substitutes for money work. Thomas, a young friend of mine, couldn't understand why his mom always said she had no money when she had a perfectly good set of cheques in her purse. He'd seen her use a cheque to pay for stuff before. So how come she couldn't do it when *he* wanted something?

If you think about all the different ways we can now pay for goods and services — by cheque, credit card, debit card or with cold hard cash — it's little wonder our children don't understand how it all works. We can go up to machines, stick in little plastic cards and out comes money. Where did it come from? Does the machine ever dry up? Maybe money doesn't grow on trees. Perhaps banks make money, since it seems their inexhaustible supply is always accessible.

One of the biggest mysteries for most people is the whole process of getting credit. Most of us have no idea how the decision is made, how a credit rating works, or the importance placed on "character" in making the decision to lend. For years we extend our children credit in the form of loans or allowance advances. Yet many parents have little or no expectation of "repayment." Children grow up thinking a loan is a way to get money you need, no strings attached.

When it comes to investments, since most people feel lost themselves, there is little chance they can shed light on this area for their kids. But the times they are a'changin'. About a year ago I received a letter from a grandmother with two teenage granddaughters who spent their summers working on the farm. The previous year, their father had invested their hard-earned money in a government bond paying a low rate of interest. The girls' friends had their summer's earnings invested in mutual funds. Her granddaughters were very disappointed with the return they earned on their investments. They felt they had worked too hard to watch their money slowly earning three percent a year, particularly since their friends' investments were doing so much better. They wanted to know more, and they were determined to make better investment decisions. They were about to start the process of becoming educated so they could take control of their own finances.

Ultimately the best we can offer our children is the knowledge and practice needed to make the best possible decisions. We won't always be able to help them with those decisions. So if we constantly assume control, we do them a disservice. It takes practice to get good at anything. And every decision doesn't bring the perfect result. We also have to learn to roll with the punches. As parents, we know there comes a point we have to let go. Might I suggest that, instead of letting go all at once, you do so a little at a time.

I recently read an article on teaching children about spending. The thrust of the article was that if you didn't believe your child was making a good buying decision with *his* money, as a parent you have the right and responsibility to veto your child's purchase. I disagree with this wholeheartedly. If we have the right of veto, we maintain both the responsibility and the accountability, and our children are off the hook. This isn't teaching.

That's not to say we can't reason with and guide our children. If your child seems hell-bent on buying something you feel will have very little value once the purchase has been made, you can suggest a breathing space. Suggest that your son think about it for a couple of days. Reassure him that should he still want that toy, book or piece of candy on Saturday, you'll be very happy to bring him back to get it. And keep your commitment. What you are trying to do is remove the undeniable influence of the magic marketers — the people who design the packaging and the product for maximum appeal and impulse buying. If in the cold reality of your living room your son still insists on his purchase, that's his decision. He will shortly find out for himself if there is value in his purchase. The next time he sees something he wants and hasn't the money to buy it, he will weigh his last purchase (you can help the process by reminding him gently — don't "I told you so" him, though) in terms of this missed opportunity.

Of course, the only way this will work is if you keep your own hands out of your pocket. Only a true consequence will teach the important lesson of value buying. Your intervention, just this one time, will eliminate his pain and mitigate any gain in terms of true learning.

One final word. All the suggestions and advice in this book are just that: suggestions and advice. You are the person who best knows your child. You'll know when a point is worth making, and when being flexible will have as positive an impact. This isn't about laying a plan and sticking to it come hell or high water. If we want our children to be able to deal with life, they are going to have to be flexible. If we want them to be flexible, we're going to have to demonstrate some flexibility of our own. Ultimately our children will learn based on what we do.

The same holds true for how we teach them about money. The best way to learn is by example. If we think of ourselves as our children's mentors, we can easily see how important it is that we learn to manage money, understand where it fits and place the proper priority on its acquisition and use.

You've watched your child mimic the way you or your spouse walks, talks, and does everything else. When Alexandra started to talk, she would ask for a bottle of water by saying, "woatah." That was the first time I heard my accent come from her lips. Each time she said, "diahpah," to indicate she wanted to be changed, my husband was on the floor in hysterics. And when I once jokingly said, "Walk this way" and started waddling down the hallway, little did I know that "Walk this way" would produce the same waddle forever after.

Our children watch us closely. They understand much more than many of us imagine. And they are very smart. They learn more in their first five years than they ever learn again. By the time they are teenagers, they've learned as much or more than we learn for the entire rest of our lives. From that point on, the learning is harder to integrate. Up until that point, we can learn so well it almost seems intuitive.

If you want your child to be intuitively smart about money, start modeling the behaviours you value. Remember that each trip to the grocery store is an opportunity to learn. Since your child will instinctively be learning — that's what children do best — wouldn't it be wise to be aware of what you are teaching?

Keep the communication open and fun. Play games, take every opportunity to teach, use the whole world as your classroom. Talk about budgeting, spending and investing openly and honestly with your children. Share your successes and celebrate your children's, no matter how small. Reward their learning, and when they seem to be wobbling off course, gently redirect them. When they make mistakes, show them how to pick themselves up, brush themselves off and get on with it. And let them assume the responsibility and accountability. Teach them to take charge and to be in control.

You can give your child no greater gift than to be *able*.

1 TEACHER, TEACHER

We learn more by looking for the answer
to a question and not finding it
than we do from learning the answer itself.
— Lloyd Alexander

If you think teaching kids about money is a difficult task, let me assure you
it's as easy as potty-training, teaching manners or developing thoughtful and
considerate children. Let's face it, you're a natural. You've been teaching your
children from the day they were born. You taught them to walk, to talk and to
use a knife and fork (although sometimes you wonder whether they may have
regressed).

Think back to the nurturing you gave when your baby started to take her
first tentative steps. You encouraged her by celebrating even her smallest
successes. You helped to take the fear away by letting her hold your hands.
You laughed and played. It was fun. And she learned to walk.

Potty-training may have seemed more arduous, but it happened. In fact, as
paediatricians often point out, there isn't a single kid in university still in
diapers. One child may progress at a slower rate than another. But it's not how
quickly you get there that counts, it's the fact that you get there. And the less
strife, tears and anger involved in the whole process, the better. Learning
should be fun. It should carry with it a sense of reward. It should feel good.

So here are some golden rules about creating an environment where
learning about money will be fun:

1. Treat your children with respect and dignity. They have to feel good about
   themselves, and about learning, for the stuff you are teaching to stick.

2. Ask lots of questions. Questions get kids thinking. Giving them the answers
   first and then testing what they remember may be the method you're most

familiar with, but it's not the best way to learn. Ask them what they think and encourage them to find the answers.

3. Suggest activities. Avoid commanding them to do exercises, play games or complete tasks. If they don't buy into the experience, they won't learn.

4. Set realistic expectations. If you or your children expect too much, you will be disappointed. Mistakes are natural and should be seen as learning tools (now that I know that doesn't work, I'll try this). Be patient and supportive. Pace yourself. Remember, the process of learning is a natural one.

5. Let your children experience the learning for themselves. Avoid jumping in to show them how. Let them experiment. Let them choose. And when you give them the opportunity to choose, follow their choices without question. Do you remember as a child hearing, "You just won't take any advice — you have to feel the pain yourself"? We all have the right to chart our own course. Learning from the natural consequences of our decisions is the best learning.

6. Listen to your children. You not only need to hear what they know, you also need to listen for what they don't know or have misunderstood.

7. Each child is an individual and has the right to learn at her own pace, in her own space. Don't compare kids. Don't criticize. Offer alternative ways of doing things. "Molly, you don't seem to be having a lot of success with that approach. Perhaps if you tried…"

8. GIVE SCADS AND SCADS OF POSITIVE REINFORCEMENT! There is no greater reward than being told how well you are doing. Say it often, but mean it when you say it. If it's just words, kids will pick up on it immediately. Be honest in your feedback. Be appreciative of their efforts. Be loving and attentive in your approach.

THE VALUE OF PLAY

While many people believe you must work hard at learning, this makes learning a chore. Play is a very effective way of learning; it's the most natural way of learning, and it allows children to try new skills, express their feelings, explore their world and practise being grown up.

Sometimes your children won't be ready to play a game you're suggesting. Try playing the game yourself. Just sit down on the floor and begin. Curiosity is a particularly strong suit in most children, and you will find they quickly join in your play, asking lots of questions.

A key to successfully creating play that's also learning is to ensure you are integrating a variety of senses into the activity. I can't begin to count the number of hours I sat and watched Alex play, slotting different shapes into a ball with the appropriately shaped holes. When I played with her, as she sorted the shapes I labeled them for her. I would say, "That's a square. A square has four sides, all even. That's a circle and it's round." When we played together with her shapes, she not only learned to slot the right shape into the right hole, she also learned the words that matched the shapes and some of the characteristics of each shape. It wasn't a matter of "fast tracking" her. I had no expectation that she would suddenly have a complete understanding of geometry. It was a matter of linking the various senses together. She felt the shapes, she heard the words. Sometimes she would repeat a word after me.

THE WORLD AS YOUR CLASSROOM

Children love to be a part of everything their parents do. Sometimes it's even difficult to get five minutes in the bathroom by ourselves. They want so much to be with us. They want to watch us. They are hungry to learn so they can be just like us.

The world offers a multitude of opportunities for teaching children. When you let your son measure out the flour, sugar, chocolate and butter for a batch of brownies, you teach about measurements. When you let your daughter count out the change at the grocery store, you're teaching her about measurements, too.

To teach children, from preschoolers to teenagers, about money we can involve them in activities we do. At the grocery store, explain what you are looking for and what has an impact on your buying decision. "Well, Molly, we're going to pick up some tinned salmon now. Oh, look, this salmon is on sale. That's thirty cents off the normal price. That's good value. I think I'll get an extra tin this week." While your child won't understand everything you're saying, she will remember the importance you place on shopping wisely.

A MATTER OF CHOICE

One of the greatest frustrations children face is that they often don't seem in control of anything. Before they can talk we feed them food without being able to determine what they like to eat. Think about it. When you're deciding on what to make for dinner, you often start by saying, "Gee, what do I feel like eating tonight?" Yet many people thrust what they feel like eating on their kids with the added threat of "Eat it all or no dessert."

Choice is important to children. When you're out shopping, involve your child in some of the shopping decisions. "Alex, would you like carrots or peas for dinner this week? Do you think we should get some of these lovely apples for Daddy? Look at those beautiful strawberries. I bet Manda would love those. What do you think?"

THE DIFFERENT STAGES OF LEARNING

There's a natural progression to the way children learn, and to a large extent it's based on physiology. As a child's brain develops, neural networks are created that are able to handle new and different types of learning. It's important to have at least a basic understanding of how we learn to appreciate the need for different types of learning environments.

This need to learn in different ways, and to adjust our teaching to the way our children can learn based on age, is the main reason this book is filled with a variety of discussion points and games. If we accept that children learn in different ways, and that at different stages of their lives their learning patterns change, then we also need to adjust how we are teaching them so we maximize the opportunities for learning available to us.

Most of what is generally known about how learning takes place was developed by a Swiss psychologist by the name of Jan Piaget who began his career around 1920. Over several decades, Piaget developed a new, and at the time somewhat radical, view of how people think.

JAN PIAGET

According to Piaget, initially babies make sense of the world by seeing the impact their physical actions have on the world. A baby shakes a rattle and realizes he can create and re-create the sound. A newborn cries and, realizing his parents will respond, cries again whenever he wants attention. Between age one and two, toddlers begin to appreciate that they exist in time and space. They learn, for example, that an object continues to exist even when they can no longer see it.

Next comes the ability to *interiorize actions*. Children's newly developed ability to imagine means they do not have to go through each stage to create the desired response. They can imagine the first two or three steps and act on the fourth, the step that actually creates the desired result. They are also now capable of symbol use. They can use words, gestures or pictures to stand for real objects, and are developing language and drawing skills.

At about seven or eight, a significant pattern shift occurs. Children's imaginations seem to become stuck, and concentration on rules and practical ideas is the norm. It is at this stage that a child can rearrange a pile of coins and know that the same quantity remains. Up to this point, a change in shape created a change in the child's perception of reality. Seven coins spread out on a table were "bigger" than seven coins stacked, so the child's typical response was that there were more coins in the "spread" than in the "stack." By the age of eight, children have usually learned to "conserve number" so that a change in shape does not necessarily mean the mass has been affected.

In early adolescence, a new stage of development comes into play. Children are able to reason about the world. They can suppose an idea, test it and revise their supposition based on this experience. It is at this stage that children are capable of "adult" logical-rational thought. Beyond this point there are no qualitative changes in a child's thinking.

HOWARD GARDNER

Howard Gardner, a prominent American psychologist, spent years observing children's creative-play development. His research showed that children's creativity has distinct forms and different needs during the different stages of their lives.

Creativity may not at first seem to have a big place in learning about money. It does. Creativity refers to things like a child's ability to shift his thinking, to use details in working out ideas, and to select and refine ideas. Creativity is a cornerstone of learning.

In his book, *Frames of Mind: The Theory of Multiple Intelligences,* Gardner observes that while the broad outlines of Piaget's development research remain of interest, stages of development are much smoother and gradual than Piaget's rigid definitions. And there is now evidence that children can conserve number, classify consistently and abandon their single-minded focus on their own needs as early as age three.

According to Gardner's research, preschool — or stage one — children are highly creative. They love music and dance, drama and language. They are uncritical observers in terms of what adults term "accomplishment." They do, and they delight in what they do. A preschooler may feel that a painting is complete when he has completely filled the paper with swirls of colour.

Seven-, eight- and nine-year-olds have entered the second stage, where they are more able to deal with literal meanings rather than metaphors. They would rather collect pictures than make their own.

The third stage develops between age 15 and 25 and coincides with Piaget's "formal operations," where the thinker can now plan, implement and evaluate a creative project.

Gardner's primary focus is on the area of intelligence. He believes strongly that we have neglected the wide range of human intelligences in favour of traditional IQ tests which in no way take these multiple intelligences into account. In essence, Gardner says that there are seven (or more) separate intelligences, which lead to different types of adult accomplishments, and that our standard tests are inadequate in measuring, or totally ignore, these intelligences. His seven intelligences are:

1. Linguistic: writers and poets
2. Logical-mathematical: mathematicians and scientists

3. Visual-spatial: pilots, architects and sculptors
4. Bodily-kinesthetic: athletes, instrumentalists, dancers and surgeons
5. Musical: composers and performers
6. Interpersonal: understanding other people
7. Intrapersonal: understanding ourselves and our personal philosophies.

While he acknowledges that there may be more intelligences than these seven, he believes that most individuals have a natural affinity for one or more of these seven. He suggests that we stop asking, "How smart is my child?" and start asking, "How is my child smart?" And he sees a strong need to move away from the traditional linguistic/logical-mathematical focus so we can recognize the artistic and personal skills.

Gardner also notes that while children cannot be expected to be equally good at all things — they will have areas of strength and weakness — their adult role models will play an important part in helping them develop, and in exciting them about learning and about making choices for their lives.

ROBERT STERNBERG

Another innovative thinker who is more concerned about how children actually solve problems than how "smart" they are, Sternberg uses three intelligence labels. Analytic intelligence is the basis on which most traditional education programs are based. Creative intelligence is the one most often ignored and has a direct impact on a child's ability to deal with a rapidly changing world. Practical intelligence is the ability to function successfully — what most of us often refer to as common sense. Each of us has more or less of each of these three intelligences, and this, according to Sternberg's research, may explain why children who do very well in school do less well in life, and vice versa.

JANE HEALY

Jane Healy, author of *A Child's Growing Mind: A Practical Guide to Brain Development and Learning from Birth to Adolescence*, is a learning specialist with a Ph.D. in educational psychology and has been a professional educator for more than 30 years. Healy's experiences coincide with many of Gardner's observations. In her book, she goes so far as to detail the types of learning that take place at each of the three stages, broken down into much smaller age groups.

Learning always involves memory, and Healy says there are strategies that can be used by children and adults alike to help remember. As your child's guide to the world of money, you may want to consider using some of these tips in your discussions with your kids.

1. We have six different senses, and each of these senses uses different parts of our brain and affects memory in different ways. As teachers we need to appeal to a child's different senses to help her remember. If we can incorporate touch, smell, sight, hearing and taste into our children's play experiences, we run a much better chance of creating a strong memory. A game, or a variety of games, that incorporates different senses will have a stronger long-term educational impact than a single game with a single sensory experience.

2. Linking new ideas to ideas already understood is a good way to build a memory. It requires your child to actively think, and it'll keep you on your toes, too. Here are a couple of examples:

   • A transit token is like a coin. Its worth is based on what it costs to ride the subway or bus. Instead of having to carry around 75 cents in change, you can use your 75 cents to buy a token, and then use that token to pay for your ride. Can you think of any other types of "currencies" that we buy to make our lives more convenient? How about traveller's cheques? What about tickets at a fair? Postage stamps?

   • A cheque is a guaranteed promise that you will pay for something you want to buy. Since you may not always want to carry lots of cash around, in case of loss or theft, you can use a cheque. When you write a cheque and sign your name on the bottom, you are promising to pay the shopkeeper for the goods you're taking with you. But it's a guaranteed promise. So you have to have the money in the bank for the amount you are writing on the cheque.

3. Showing patterns by categorizing. For example, pennies, nickels, dimes and quarters are all coins. Certificates of deposits, stocks and bonds are all types of investments.

4. Elaborating by linking information together. Examples of elaborating include making up a story using the new words or concepts, creating an acronym or drawing a picture to represent the ideas. "When you get to the store, Max, remember you want to buy a moose: milk, oranges, oatmeal, sugar and eggs."

5. Creating logical connections between events. Even a three-year old remembers things better when they seem logical. "Molly, if there are five pennies in a nickel, and there are two nickels in a dime, how many pennies are there in a dime?" Healy acknowledges that sometimes it can be difficult to get impulsive children to go through the logical connections themselves. She offers five questions you can use to help your child get, and stay, focused.
   - What do you have to do?
   - How do you think you should go about doing it?
   - What will you need to do first?
   - Are you following your plan?
   - Did you finish what you had to do?

6. Rehearsing builds familiarity with a new concept or skill. We've all heard it before: practice makes perfect. According to Healy, "an activity must be repeated many times to firm up neural networks for proficiency. Repetition isn't boring for young children." It's a good idea to do lots of rehearsal to establish skills and firm up new ideas and to refresh memory. Rehearsal can be accomplished by physically repeating the steps ("Max, would you count out the change for me") or imagining the process ("Molly, how much change would you give me?")

THE TALKING/THINKING LINK

A lot of research has been done on the linkages between families who talk thoughtfully about issues and the development of children's abilities to think. In families where conversation abounds, children are better readers, writers and reasoners.

The development of inner speech is key to the ability to problem-solve, plan, comprehend and build memory. The best way to help children develop the ability to think is to talk with them. The *with* is important. Many people confuse talking *at* and talking *with*. Talking *at* serves little purpose other than to bore the pants off kids. There's no sharing of ideas, just straight one-way communication. Remember what it felt like as a child when an adult launched into a full explanation of a topic you were only slightly interested in? Adults still do this to each other, and the result is a glazing over of the eyes as the listener waits patiently for the lecture to end.

On the other hand, talking *with* your children can help them learn to figure things out, develop creative — if sometimes a little unusual — solutions, and become independent thinkers and reasoners. And the single most effective tool in talking with is the *open* question. An open question is one that offers your child the opportunity to imagine, to wonder and to answer in detail.

- What would happen if all the money in the world suddenly disappeared?
- What would you do if you had three wishes?
- Why do you think you need an allowance?

The opposite of an open question is a *closed* question. These questions usually only require a yes or no answer, a short, straightforward response or a choice between two alternatives.

- Do you understand?
- How many nickels in a dime?
- Do you think $5 a week is enough, or do you need more?

Salespeople know the value of an open question: it lets the buyer talk. There's no quick answer, so thought is required for the response. And because the buyer does a lot of talking, the salesperson has the opportunity to learn a lot about what's important to the buyer.

Conversing with kids is no different. To learn about them — and help them learn — you need to hear how they think so you can observe as their minds go through the somersaults of reasoning.

Now, as most salespeople know well, open questions don't always elicit a bountiful response. It's all in the positioning. Ask an open question at the wrong time and you'll be faced with a gaping mouth and furrowed brow. All the person's body language will be saying is, "Huh? Where did that come from?" The same is true for using open questions with your kids. There has to be a framework for the question, and the questions have to flow naturally from one to another. The development of productive shared conversation will be best achieved when, as the conversation guide, you use a combination of open and closed questions.

The use of these two types of questions may not, at first, come completely naturally. Sales trainers and writers of sales books have made millions weaving mystery around the area of how to question effectively. But this questioning skill is really not that difficult to develop. It takes a bit of practice, but the effort is worth it. You'll find that as your ability to help your children see different perspectives develops, so will your ability to help your co-workers, customers, and friends — in fact, anyone with whom you interact — see from different perspectives.

Since children tend to model their thinking after that of their parents and teachers, to develop children who are strong at reasoning and creative thinking, we need to show them how to use their minds in flexible ways. We also have to demonstrate that they should not be afraid of taking intellectual risks. New, outrageous and nontraditional ideas can all seem pretty risky. But if you're not afraid to entertain weird and wonderful thoughts, neither will your children be. That's not to say that "right" and "wrong" answers are thrown out the window. But the objective in talking with kids is to create a safe place for curious thinking. Responses such as "I hadn't thought about it like that, but let me see..." and "I'm not sure how that would work, let me think..." show children that it's perfectly fine not to come up with the one right answer. These responses give credence to their thoughts, while allowing you to continue to guide the conversation in a positive direction. They are not only kinder (as opposed to "That's the stupidest thing I've ever heard!"), they

11

build trust and allow children to brave new areas that, because of their lack of experience, they might otherwise avoid (for fear of hearing, "That's the stupidest thing I've ever heard!").

In guiding conversations with children, you want to help them develop the ability to generate lots of ideas and shift easily from one idea to another. Originality should always count. That means everyone participating in the conversation must suspend judgement. Since the whole objective is to avoid functional fixedness (i.e., always sticking to the tried-and-true solutions), judgement responses need to shown the door, and brainstorming techniques that help children step beyond the known boundaries need to be encouraged.

It is important to note here that adults and children reason differently. Children tend to be concrete, relying on their experience and personal associations. Adults can be abstract since their physical brain has developed many more connections based on their much wider base of learning experiences. The younger the child, the harder it is for them to deal with abstracts. You need to get in tune with your child's level of reasoning. Up until about age five, children are very self-centred. They believe that everyone sees the world from their perspective. Since they have difficulty generalizing situations outside their own experience, they are usually too young to use "conversational" and conceptual learning. Prior to age five, the majority of your money lessons should, therefore, be focused on familiarizing your child with the *idea* of money.

One way to beginning building money skills at this early age is to give your child money to pay for a treat. An ice-cream cone may cost three quarters. Give the child the money and allow her to count out the correct number of coins on the counter. If change is due, ask the salesperson to give the change directly to your child. The objective of this lesson is that money has value and can be traded for other things of value. It also reinforces that the money has to be given in order to receive the treat.

You can practise at home by setting up a little store where your child is the salesperson. Choose several toys, label them with prices and go shopping. You can then pay your child and take your treasure home!

Playing with coins is also a good way to start your child on the road to mathematical wizardry. Practise counting using coins.

Between age five and seven, children begin to make the transition to conceptual thinking. But they still base their reasoning on personal

12

experience. If they've had an experience, they'll be able to talk about it. If they haven't yet had any experience with the topic, they may just choose to observe the conversation.

At this age, children understand that money is needed to buy things and that different things cost different amounts of money. It is at this point that you want to begin to create an understanding that money is not limitless, and therefore, you must carefully choose what you'll spend your money on. Saving for a purchase (a small one) will begin the development of this understanding. Remember, however, that the best teacher is experience itself. If your child decided to save three dollars to buy a book, but decided when she had $2.25 to spend it on candy, that's her decision. You can point out the consequences. "Molly, you've saved for three weeks for the book. If you spend your money now on the candy, you'll have to save a long time again to have enough for the book. What's more important to you — having the candy now, or being able to get the book next weekend when you get your next allowance?"

If Molly chooses to blow her stash, that's her decision. It's her money. If she wails to get the book next weekend when she's back to only 75 cents, it's your job to let the real consequence — and learning — have its impact. Don't give in. If you do, you may be sending the message that, yes, money does grow on trees, and Mommy or Daddy are money-tree harvesters.

At this age, you can start using coins for simple mathematical calculations. How many cents are there in a nickel? Practise exchanging the correct number of pennies for a higher-value coin. Point out that each coin is marked so that your child can quite easily tell how many pennies he should be giving or getting during the exchange.

From about age seven to about 12, children become more able to reason ideas. They move from the rigidity of their previous thinking to a broader ability to imagine themselves in different situations. Since they are in the concrete stage of development, they will appreciate the ability to be in charge of the conversation from time to time.

At this stage, your child will have more of the patience necessary — and can save for a longer period — to accomplish a goal. She should also be developing the ability to make appropriate choices about how to spend her money, and can begin to understand how the banking system works. Helping children learn to budget and make appropriate purchasing decisions is important at this stage. One neat game involves assigning your child a specific amount of imaginary money, and then having her decide what she wants to buy with her money using a store catalogue.

From about age 12 onward, children begin to refine their ideas about the world and to experiment with ethical thinking. As their independence grows, they will pull away, seeking to develop their own identities. They will appreciate sharing ideas and activities where you jointly seek the answers to questions.

Older children can participate in family budgeting decisions. For example, if it's time for a family treat, you can tell your kids how much money you have and let them help decide how it should be spent. (We can go to the movies, or we can go to the park and then stop at a favourite restaurant, or we can go to the museum and then stop for an ice-cream cone on the way home.)

THE ROLE OF LANGUAGE

How good are you at dealing with the semantics of language? Language is one of the most difficult of all skills to master. As teachers, we need to be very aware of how our children are using language, and how they are applying it to their reasoning.

Here's a great example of a language/reasoning flub. As my friend's daughter stood at the door ready to leave for school she said, "It's raining outside because I put on my coat." How would you respond? It's important to watch for language/reasoning confusion so that you can help guide your child through the correct reasoning. "Was it raining before you put your coat on? If it was sunny outside and you put on your coat, would that make it rain?"

As your child experiences (through the learning games in this book), ask her to retell her experience so that she can apply the appropriate language (and you can check the reasoning). "Why don't you tell Daddy about how you sorted the coins into piles today." Since children remember better when they say it themselves, this will not only allow you to check her language/ reasoning relationship and check her understanding, it will also serve as reinforcement of the learning.

It's okay to use words your child may not yet be familiar with, as long as you do so in a context that is familiar. When you use an unfamiliar term, draw your child's attention to it. ("There's a special word for that kind of coin. It's called a dime.") If you are teaching about relative terms (a nickel is bigger than a penny), demonstrate what you are saying. "This nickel is bigger than this penny. Which is bigger, the nickel or the quarter?"

PUTTING IT ALL TOGETHER

It doesn't matter what age your child is; if you haven't started talking about how money works and the role it will play in your child's future, now is the right time to start. Because children learn differently at different stages of their development, the exercises included in the following chapters are labelled for different age levels — there's something for everyone — with concrete, hands-on games for the younger, highly experiential learner to thoughtful discussions for the older, more abstract thinkers.

The age guides are *guides* only. Children develop at remarkably different rates, and you need to test where you child is to determine the tools that will bring the lesson home in the most enjoyable and effective way. As a parent, you already know the value of flexibility. And if you have more than one child, you know just how different they are in how they like to learn. You're the best judge of your child's stage of development. If you try a particular exercise and your child seems bored, move to an exercise for older children and see how she responds. If you think you've started at a level a little too high because your child just isn't responding, move to an exercise for a younger child and see how that works. As a teacher, you have to be flexible, and you need to keep watching to see how your child responds.

SOME FINAL TIPS

- Don't solve problems for your children. Avoid the urge to rush in and demonstrate. Ask questions rather than launching into an explanation. (Child says, "The door won't close." Parent, seeing the toy in the doorjamb, asks, "Is there anything blocking the door?" as opposed to, "There's a toy in the door. I'll move it and then you'll be able to close the door.") When your child asks a question, respond with a question that is just hard enough to make her think. Let her figure it out. Be her guide.

- If you ask a question and your child doesn't respond within about ten seconds, repeat the question. If that doesn't work, trying rephrasing it.

- Use experience to teach. Remember to first determine your child's frame of reference for a new experience. If you want to teach your child how to sort piles of coins into nickels, dimes and quarters, you may need to start teaching "classification" with something more familiar. Let your child help you sort the laundry into piles of pants, shirts and towels. Let him sort the groceries as you're unpacking them — here's a pile for tins, one for boxes and one for vegetables and fruits. Begin by teaching a concept with tools or items that are familiar. Once the concept of classification has been experienced, he will be better able to understand how coins can also be sorted.

- Involve your child's imagination — provide materials that can be used to build a coin collector rather than buying a piggy bank.

- Help your child to break down a problem into manageable steps.
  - What do you have to do?
  - How do you think you should go about doing it?
  - What will you need to do first?
  - Are you following your plan?
  - Did you finish what you had to do?

- Compliment your child.
  - You did a great job with that. I bet you're pretty pleased.
  - That's an interesting-looking drawing. Tell me about it.
  - You certainly seem to have enjoyed making balls from that clay.

- Don't be frustrated by "I forget." A child's inability to remember means that the learning hasn't firmed up yet. More practice is needed to integrate the learning.

- If you don't know the answer to a question or problem, say so. Go in search of the answer together. Use this as an opportunity to show your child how you ask questions to find answers. Together, you can share your learning.

- Remember that understanding is learned. You can create the right circumstances and help your child in developing understanding, but you can't teach understanding. Your child has to be ready and she has to do it herself. And without understanding, real learning hasn't taken place. Be tolerant of wrong answers and let your child explore to develop her understanding.

- Don't take your teaching responsibility so seriously that you wear your child out. Remember, learning should be fun. Incessant stimulation, on the other hand, can be a headache. Children need quiet time to process new information and to allow their brains to form new connections. (I've often felt that those deep, faraway stares are just our brain-computers shutting down for a few seconds to process new information.) Constructive playtime should be relaxed and pressure-free. Learning begins only after a child feels comfortable and familiar in a setting. And as long as an activity is holding your child's interest, let the play continue. Avoid the trap of switching activities too quickly or too often.

On a final note: while I stress the importance of allowing for creativity, not being judgemental, sharing ideas, letting kids lead the learning, letting go of some of the structure, no right or wrong answers and all the rest, I still believe that some structure is important. Children need discipline and structure so they have the security to explore. Creativity and structure aren't (pardon the pun) the opposite sides of a coin. They work together. As your child's guide, teacher, parent, most ardent admirer and greatest fan, it is up to you to determine the appropriate balance.

Now, let's get to the fun!

2 MONEY 101

Imagine a world where there is no money. Many of us sometimes feel that the world would be better off without it. Money seems to cause strife, instil fear and create greed. But there's no substitute for money when it comes to smooth and convenient trade.

Before the invention of money, if we needed something we didn't grow or make, we bartered. We exchanged what we had for what we needed. But barter wasn't always easy or convenient. Numerous trades often had to be made so that all parties would end up with something of value to them. It isn't always convenient to have a couple eggs in your pocket when you want to pick up a pack of gum. And who's to say how many eggs are worth a package of gum anyway?

Out of sheer necessity, money was invented.

DISCUSSION POINTS

If you were a farmer and there was no such thing as money, what might you use to buy the things you want, like toys, bubblegum and comic books?
If you were a carpenter, what would you use?
If you were a baker, what would you use?
If you were a schoolteacher, what would you use?
If you were a clown, what would you use?

WHO INVENTED MONEY?

Money didn't start out as coins and pieces of paper. Money started as different things in different countries. Some people used beads, others used shiny stones. The people on the island of Yap in the Pacific Ocean used stoned wheels carved from rock from the Beleau Islands, more than 300 miles away. These stones were 12 feet tall and weighed more than 500 pounds. On the island of Santa Cruz, people used feathers as money. Sharks' teeth, shells and braids of hair have all been used as money. It really doesn't matter what the money is made of; as long as people agree that a certain item is money, then that's what it is.

Thousands of years ago, people began to use lumps of metal as money. Rare metals such as gold and silver were most often chosen because of their inherent value. But the process was complicated since these metals had to be weighed. And the scales weren't always balanced in favour of the buyer.

In about 700 B.C., the king of Lydia (where Turkey is today) began to mould metal into shapes, weighing each coin and marking them with images to identify their worth. Kings often get their way, and the first coins as we know them today were created. The word "money" comes from the Latin *moneta,* the name of the place in ancient Rome where money was first made and stored.

Of course, carrying around all those coins was as much a problem then as it is now. To save the backache, people deposited their coins with trustworthy souls — monks or goldsmiths — who would give them a slip of paper that identified the value of the coins. Voilà — paper currency. The Chinese were using paper money as far back as A.D. 1275.

Fun with Money ——————————— Age 10+

A toymaker has toys but wants to build a doghouse. A baker can bake cakes but wants a new pair of shoes. The carpenter can build a doghouse, but needs a quart of milk. The milkman has milk, but wants to buy a cake for his daughter's birthday. The shoemaker has shoes, but wants to buy a toy for the milkman's daughter's birthday. How many trades will the baker have to make to get a new pair of shoes?

DISCUSSION POINT
Can you think of anything that is not money but that we use like money?
Transit tokens, traveller's cheques, tickets at a fair, postage stamps.

WHO MAKES MONEY?

Each country makes its own money, and money is made at a place called the mint. Coins are made by heating metal and pressing it into thin sheets that are then cut into blank coins — much like cookies being cut from a sheet of dough. Paper money is made of special paper and has intricate designs to discourage counterfeiters. The images that appear on a paper bill are usually carved into steel plates that are then used to create the impressions that distinguish one denomination from another, and one currency from another. Some paper bills have special markings that are extremely difficult to duplicate, while others use thin strips of metal embedded into the paper. All these special steps are taken to thwart counterfeiters and maintain the integrity of the currency.

Fun with Money ———————————— Age 3+

Children can make their own coins using modelling clay or dough. Roll out the clay or dough, then let the kids cut out "coins" using different shapes. They can then label the different coins by drawing on designs, adding stickers or using shiny stones to decorate their coins before they're allowed to dry.

A DOLLAR BY ANY OTHER NAME

In the eighteenth century, money was referred to as "rhino"; in the early nineteenth century as "mint drops" and in the 1940s as "moolah." One of the most enduring names for money — "buck" — originated in about 1850, and the term "big bucks" invaded everyday conversation in the 1970s. The word "dough" has been around for about as long as "buck" and may have caught on because everyone *kneads* it. Many terms for money developed based on the names of metals used to make them: "brass" was popular before 1600, and before 1850 "pewter" was popular. Today, our "nickel" is a holdover from the days when nickel was the primary metal used in minting five-cent coins.

Have you ever wondered where the term "two bits" comes from? The Spanish had a coin worth eight reals (former unit of currency in Spain) that became known in the Americas as the Spanish dollar. Because it was soft, when a person needed to make change, he could simply chop the coin into halves and then into quarters. A half was called "four bits" and a quarter was called "two bits."

DISCUSSION POINTS

How many different names can you think of for money?

Bread, moolah, dough, bucks, smackers, boodle, wad, long green, shekels, scratch, loot, gravy, simoleons, lettuce, ducats, kale.

If you invented your own money, what would you call it? Why?

Fun with Money ——————— Age 4+

Once your child becomes somewhat familiar with coins, try this game. Lay a penny, nickel, dime and quarter on the table. Ask your child to point to each coin as you give directions (Touch the penny. Now touch the quarter).

Next, tell your child to turn around. Remove one of the coins. Ask him to turn back and identify which coin is missing.

Remember to praise him if he's right. If he' wrong, show him the coin.

Fun with Money ——————————— Age 4+

Give your child money to buy something from a machine when you next go to the store. Let her put the money in and learn to operate the machine.

Show your preschooler how to operate a pay phone. Give her a quarter and let her call Grandma, Daddy or Mommy at work, or a friend.

Show your child how to put the current change in a newspaper box and take a newspaper. (This might open up a discussion on why it is appropriate to take only one newspaper.)

Fun with Money ——————————— Age 5+

Have your child collect an example of each coin used in your currency. Help him do rubbings of the front and back of each coin by placing a piece of paper over the coin and rubbing lightly with a crayon or pencil until the image of the coin appears. (A variation with more sparkle is to use foil papers for the rubbings. Use a firm object to rub over the foil and create embossings.) Talk about what distinguishes one coin from another. Focus on how we can easily recognize coins when we become familiar with their markings.

Collect coins of other currencies, make rubbings of them and have your child build his own coin library.

Give your child an opportunity to spend some of his money. Turn your kitchen into a restaurant and let your child "buy" a glass of juice, a sandwich and a cookie for lunch.

Fun with Money ———————— Age 6+

Once your child is completely familiar with coins, introduce her to paper money. One denomination at a time, show her how many pennies, nickels, dimes and quarters it takes to equal a dollar, and then the face value of the paper money you are using. Your objective is to demonstrate how difficult it would be to carry around, for example, twenty dollars worth of pennies.

Have your child create paper money of her own. Then set up shop and let her go shopping. First let her pay for an item with coins. Then let her pay for it with her paper money.

Fun with Money ———————— Age 8+

For children who have addition and subtraction skills, let them practise making change from paper bills. Use actual paper money and coins to help reinforce how to make change. For example:

- "I want to give you a dollar, but I only have a five-dollar bill. How much change will you have to give me?"

- "Here's a ten-dollar bill. I need to get back at least four quarters and five dimes. But I want as much of it in paper as possible. How would you make change?"

- "Here's a five-dollar bill. If I give you 25 cents, how much change would you give me?"

┌─ **fun with Money** ─────────────── **Age 12+** ─┐

Older children can be asked to conceptualize this exercise.

- "If you had ten dollars and wanted to buy a item for 50 cents, how much change should you receive?"

- "If you had a five-dollar bill and asked someone at a bank to change it all into quarters, how many coins should you receive?"

TIPS FOR RECEIVING CHANGE

Once kids begin to handle money, it is important they realize that it's their responsibility to keep that money safe. That includes making sure they get the right change when they pay for an item. By practising at home, you and your child can become confident she can make change accurately and quickly, and she can then set out shopping on her own. You may wish to supervise the first dozen or so expeditions so you can watch her in the real world. After that, she's on her own.

Here are some tips you should give your kids about making sure they receive the right amount of change:

- When you hand the cashier money, say out loud how much you are giving him. "Here's ten dollars."

- Keep your eye on the register and check the amount the cashier enters.

- Count your change in sight of the cashier before you leave the counter.

- If there has been a discrepancy, tell the cashier immediately. Be polite. Anyone can make a mistake. You may have added incorrectly, or the item may be incorrectly ticketed.

- If you cannot resolve the problem with the cashier, ask to speak to the manager. Politely and unemotionally, explain the situation and ask the manager to resolve the issue. The manager has the option of balancing the cash in the register to see if there is too much money in the till. But be aware that this can be very time-consuming. However, if a large enough amount is involved, it's worth it.

- If none of this works, write a letter to the president of the company. Be sure to include the exact date and the amount of the transaction (including what you purchased, the price and how much you gave the cashier), as well as a copy of your receipt.

If you think any of these steps are extreme, consider this: how will your child learn to be independent if she allows herself to be intimidated and doesn't stand up for what's right and fair? The way your child learns to deal with situations such as when she is given incorrect change reflects the way you deal with similar situations. If you remain cool and insist on the situation being rectified, she will learn that a cool head and determination will likely result in a positive resolution.

DISCUSSION POINTS
What would you do if a cashier gave you too much change?
What would it mean for the cashier if the mistake wasn't caught?

HOW MONEY IS VALUED

All money is not created equal. The value of an American dollar is different from the value of a Canadian dollar or an Australian dollar. There are lots of different types of currencies in the world and each one has a different value.

DISCUSSION POINT

How many different types of currency can you think of ?
**French franc, German mark, Japanese yen, Indian rupee, Swiss
franc, Italian lira, British pound, Dutch gilder, Mexican peso,
Austrian schilling, Brazilian real, Danish krone, Greek drachma,
Polish zloty, South African rand, Thai baht, Venezuelan bolivar,
Chinese renminbi.**

Fun with Money ——————————— Age 10+

On the next page is a word-search puzzle. Feel free to photocopy this
page. All the words to be found are names of currencies or types of
money. Many have the country included in the search (e.g., French
franc), others do not. As a separate exercise, you can ask your kids to
research where the currencies with no country name come from (e.g.,
Where is the shekel used? Which country uses a punt? Which uses a
ringgit?)

The value of money in any country is, to a large extent, based on how much
money is in circulation. The more money created, the less value the currency
has. Devaluation of a currency refers to when a country decides to print more
money in order to put more money into circulation. Since there is a greater
supply of money, the money is worth less or "devalued." So the value of
money is affected by demand and supply. As with any "collectable," the less
there is available, the more each item is worth. However, other economic
factors also affect how much money is worth. Foreign investment is one such
factor. The more foreign investment in a country, the less that country's
currency tends to be worth.

Inflation is another factor that affects the value of money. Inflation refers to
the fact that prices are rising, usually because there is too much money
available (too much supply, not enough demand). The higher the inflation, the

WORD SEARCH
CURRENCIES OF THE WORLD

```
S  O  U  T  H  A  F  R  I  C  A  N  R  A  N  D  L  E  U
P  E  V  H  P  E  S  C  N  A  R  F  H  C  N  E  R  F  M
A  N  E  A  C  R  D  E  D  A  N  I  S  H  K  R  O  N  E
N  T  L  I  H  E  S  W  I  S  S  F  R  A  N  C  A  E  X
I  R  N  B  I  T  H  A  A  R  I  L  N  A  I  L  A  T  I
S  A  A  A  N  R  E  A  N  U  R  O  K  H  C  E  Z  C  C
H  N  I  H  E  A  K  R  R  I  Y  A  L  Y  N  N  E  P  A
P  I  R  T  S  U  E  D  U  T  C  H  G  I  L  D  E  R  N
E  D  A  S  E  Q  L  D  P  R  I  N  G  G  I  T  N  U  P
S  N  G  S  R  G  R  E  E  K  D  R  A  C  H  M  A  L  E
E  A  L  N  E  Y  E  S  E  N  A  P  A  J  C  E  N  T  S
T  I  U  T  N  Q  G  Y  T  O  L  Z  H  S  I  L  O  P  O
A  R  B  T  M  R  U  S  S  I  A  N  R  U  B  L  E  A  O
S  E  G  N  I  L  L  I  H  C  S  N  A  I  R  T  S  U  A
S  G  V  E  N  E  Z  U  E  L  A  N  B  O  L  I  V  A  R
S  L  E  E  B  L  A  E  R  N  A  I  L  I  Z  A  R  B  A
Z  A  M  B  I  A  N  K  W  A  C  H  A  D  O  L  L  A  R
```

FRENCH FRANC
SHEKEL
JAPANESE YEN
SWISS FRANC
POUND
PENNY
MEXICAN PESO
BRAZILIAN REAL
GREEK DRACHMA
SOUTH AFRICAN RAND
THAI BAHT
RINGGIT
VENEZUELAN BOLIVAR
ALGERIAN DINAR
DIME
CZECH KORUNA
SPANISH PESETA

RUSSIAN RUBLE
PUNT
INDIAN RUPEE
ITALIAN LIRA
RIYAL
DUTCH GILDER
AUSTRIAN SCHILLING
DANISH KRONE
POLISH ZLOTY
DOLLAR
CENT
LEU
CHINESE RENMINBI
BULGARIAN LEV
QUARTER
ZAMBIAN KWACHA

less money is worth. That's because it takes more money to buy the same goods and services.

Fun with Money ———————————— Age 7+

To show how prices rise over time, have your child do some research on how much things cost in previous years. You can use the work sheet on the following page or make your own.

The amount of foreign trade also has an impact on the value of money. When one country buys products made in another country, it usually has to pay for those products in the currency of the country it is buying from, so money has to be exchanged. For example, when we buy cars made in Japan, we have to pay for those cars in Japanese yen. To do so, we first have to use our money to buy yen. If we are buying a lot of products from Japan, then we also have to buy a lot of yen. This creates demand for the yen, so the value of the yen goes up. This means it then takes more of our dollars to buy yen (and that makes Japanese goods more expensive). Of course, if we decide we won't buy Japanese cars anymore, we won't need to buy yen. Since the demand for yen will fall, so will the value of the yen. (Governments often stop the value of their currency from falling by buying their own currency.)

The buying and selling of currency is done through the foreign-exchange market where people trade money of different currencies. When one currency is being exchanged for another — when we use a dollar to buy, for example, a Japanese yen — the currencies' exchange rate comes into play. The exchange rate is the amount of one currency that is equal to another. The exchange rate keeps changing based on the amount of the currency in supply.

PRICES JUST KEEP GOING UP!

When my grandmother was a child...

    a loaf of bread cost   _____
    a doll cost   _____
    a house cost   _____

When my mother was a child...

    a loaf of bread cost   _____
    a doll cost   _____
    a house cost   _____

Today...

    a loaf of bread costs   _____
    a doll costs   _____
    a house costs   _____

DISCUSSION POINTS

If you bought ten dollars' worth of marbles (baseball cards or POGS) today, and sold them tomorrow for 15 dollars, you'd make a profit of five dollars. Well, currency can be bought and sold the same way.

If you buy currency today and it has a higher exchange rate tomorrow, would you make a profit? If you buy currency today and it has a lower exchange rate tomorrow, would you make a profit? If the exchange rate fell but you didn't want to lose any money, what could you do?

3 MONEY & VALUE

One of the first things children do as soon as they have some money is spend it. After all, that's what money's for, right? And people — kids and adults — spend money on the darnedest things: pet rocks and funerals for pet rocks, the invisible dog (which you can take for a walk, but never have to stoop and scoop for), bubble pack sold as "stress relief," and make-believe car phones, which allow you to keep up with the Yuppies with minimal cost.

You only have to look at how consumer-oriented our society has become to see just how big a part spending plays in our lives, children's included. According to estimates by Children's Market Research, kids in the U.S. spend more than $7 billion a year from their own resources — specifically allowance. When handouts and specific-purpose funds (grocery, video, toys, clothes and sporting goods) are taken into account, it's estimated that their total spending in the U.S. alone is more than $150 billion. The influence children have over purchases made with family dollars is also significant. Ninety percent of children influence the brand of cold cereal purchased. And 60 percent of kids between the ages of six and 14 also have a significant influence on family purchases of big-ticket items such as vacations, computers and even cars.

A number of factors have contributed to the economic role children now play, not the least of which are the changes at home and at work that have given children more responsibility and power. From buying groceries to cooking meals, our kids are more independent than previous generations'.

If you think our children are paying the price for their parents' obsession with career, think again! Research done by *Parents* magazine shows that parents are very traditional, spending more time with their kids than often they are given credit for. And we are not trying to buy our children. Parents worry most about giving their kids "the necessities in life" along with "a good education"; teaching values, instilling respect and providing religious instruction are all well ahead of gratifying kids' material desires.

Our children are growing up responsible, self-confident and capable. In fact, when surveyed, many of our kids indicate they do not feel burdened and see their participation as necessary for the family to function smoothly.

Since spending is a significant part of money management, it makes sense to try to help kids figure out the best ways to use their money. The fact that nobody taught us about smart consuming is evident in the way many people abuse "plastic." More than half of North America's credit-card holders have balances owing, paying what can be exorbitant interest rates on products and services that may not even outlive their repayment schedules. While our values are very different from our parents' — who typically spent only what they had — our "spenditis" is in large part because the money game has changed. It is in our generation that credit cards have become currency. And the statistics on credit-card usage and balances are staggering. At the end of 1994, Canadians had more than $15.4 billion in outstanding balances on MasterCard and Visa combined.

Whether we are aware of it or not, we already play an important role in teaching our kids how to be consumers. Each time we go shopping, we model what a consumer should look like. Whether the model is a positive one or not, our children are learning. Teaching our children about becoming smart consumers may mean looking closely at our own spending patterns and developing some new habits. Teaching our children also requires that we take an active role in explaining what we are doing and why.

Some of our customs, such as tipping, are not inherently self-explanatory. To a child, money left on a table with no explanation may translate into carelessness. You've paid the bill, so what's the money on the table for? Many people throw the change from their pockets into a container where it sits and accumulates. Others leave change lying around. In my household, I'm the only person who considers dimes, nickels and pennies to be currency. And I'm welcome to this unearned wealth because the rest of my family considers change a nuisance. An example of this is how my change pot continued to remain full despite my best attempts to redistribute the wealth. On special occasions I've suggested to my stepdaughter that she empty our change pot to supplement her holiday purchases. She, in turn, traded it back to her dad for real money (paper money), and the quarters, dimes, nickels and pennies returned to the change pot for me to spend. Some people think a quarter is worth more than five nickels because it's simply more convenient. It's not. Twenty-five cents is 25¢, regardless of its form. We have to be very careful that the message "change isn't real money" doesn't filter to our children.

Fun with Money ———————— Age 8+

Depending on your child's age, you might change the dollar amount in this game to an amount that will seem large to your child. For example, while an eight-year-old may think a hundred dollars is a lot, a fourteen-year-old may be more impressed with a thousand dollars.

Assemble a variety of catalogues and merchandising flyers that have products of interest to your child. Younger children will be mostly interested in toys. Older children will also be interested in catalogues for clothing, furniture, books and electronics.

Give your child the catalogues and flyers you have assembled, and ask her to make a wish list based on the statement, "If I had $100 / $1000, I would buy ..."

Talk about the wish list, asking questions such as:

• Which of the things on your list are the most important to you?

• Do you really need (identify a specific item on the list), or will you be bored with it tomorrow?

• Is there anything else you wanted that you could not get because the money ran out? How important is it to you? Would you give up anything on your current list to get this item?

• Can you get (an item from the list) cheaper somewhere else? How would you find out if it was less expensive somewhere else?

• Have you actually seen (an item from the list), touched it, played with it, tried it on? Would you order it from a catalogue or shop for it in person? Why?

* If you spent all your money now, what would you do if you saw something you really liked a lot better tomorrow?

Keep your child's list. It will come in handy for future exercises or the next special occasion.

WHERE DOES ALL THE MONEY GO?

What does a billion dollars look like? How many rooms would a billion dollar bills fill? How much would it weigh? The word *billion* has come into common usage, having much the same sense of importance that, only a few decades ago, the word *million* had. And as times keep changing, hot on the heals of billion comes *trillion*. Since most of us have never seen a million dollars all in one place, never mind a billion or a trillion, it's pretty hard to conceive of just how much money that is.

It's no different for children. Dealing with dimes and quarters is little preparation for the concept of a hundred dollars or a thousand dollars. When they see us spend a thousand dollars on an item, it might as well be a million.

BUT I NEED A NEW DOLL

The way we use language has an impact on the values we impart to our children. You've probably heard a child say, "But Mom, I need it," referring to the latest toy or trendy item of clothing. But what exactly does *need* mean? When it comes to spending money, a need is simply the motivation for your decision to buy or not to buy. Salespeople know that a need takes many forms.

- First there are the *wants,* which come about because you simply don't have something right now. It's the need to remedy the lack of a specific item or a state. I want a new doll. I want a new pair of runners. I want to be left alone.

- Next there are the *concerns.* These relate to things we worry about. I'm concerned about keeping my money safe, so I need a bank account. I'm worried about how my friends will see me, so I need the latest fashion item. I'm worried I won't pass my exam, so I need some extra coaching.

- Then there are the *problems.* Something has happened that has created a need. My bike is too small for me, so I need a new one. My car just died, so

I need a loan to buy a new car. I'm not doing well in school, so I need a tutor.

- Finally, there are the *desires*. These are the "I wish I had" or "I wish I could have" statements. I wish I could take the kids to Disney World. I wish I could buy a new coat. I wish you would listen to me.

The distinctions between these types of needs are not always easy to see. Even professional salespeople have difficulty distinguishing between a want, concern, problem or desire. But there are differences, and the differences relate to value.

Don't get me wrong. Sometimes it's perfectly appropriate to get something just because you want it. I collect hippos. I buy them because I want them. They don't satisfy any concern or problem and it's not a matter of desire. It's straight out want. I have no goal in buying a hippo, except for the gratification it brings. I have quite the hippo collection, but if I see another one I like, I'll probably buy it just because I want it.

Understanding the motivation to buy goes a long way in determining the value of the purchase. Children need to understand the subtle differences between what they want, what they are concerned about, what they may have a problem with, and what they desire. Without understanding the motivation for buying, people will inappropriately place the same value on one purchase as on another. That hinders their ability to judge the appropriateness of the buying decision.

Here's an example of a conversation between a father and his son over the decision to buy a new bike:

"Dad, I need a new bike."
"A new bike?"
"Yeah, the one I have is just too small."
"Okay, so you need a bigger bike. What have you got in mind?"
"Michael has a Z189754 Mountain Ranger Model. It's really neat. I want one of those."
"What do you think a bike like that costs?"
"A lot, but Michael's dad bought him one for his birthday."

35

"That may be so, but your mom and I just don't have that kind of money right now, so I think you should look at some other bikes."

"Awww Dad, if we go buying some cheap-o bike, all the kids will laugh at me."

"So this bike has to stand up to the approval of your friends, too?"

"Well, I don't want them thinking I'm a dweeb or somethin'. "

"Do all your friends ride this super-bike?"

"No. But they all think Michael's bike is real cool, and if I have a bike like his, they'll think I'm cool, too."

"What type of bike does David have?"

"He has an okay bike. But it's nowhere near as cool as Michael's."

"Tell me again why you need a new bike. I've forgotten."

"My bike's too small."

"So you need a bigger bike to solve the problem that your bike's too small, right?"

"I guess."

"You wish you could have a bike like Michael's, but we both know that's not something we can afford right now. So what are our options?"

"Well, I guess I'll just have to take whatever dweeby bike you decide to buy me."

"Or I could buy you no bike at all, and then you won't have a dweeby bike to contend with."

"But how will I get to school if I don't have a bike?"

"So you need a bigger bike, and if you don't get a bike you'll have a problem getting to school?"

"Yeah. I'd have to leave for school 20 minutes earlier to get there on time."

"So what do you suggest?"

"Well ... I have some money saved up from my birthday. And Grams just sent me ten dollars. Suppose I put in my money — could we get the Z189754?"

"I don't know. If I put in $70, which is what I can afford right now, would that be enough?"

"No."

"Do you have any other ideas then? Remember, you need the bike to get to school, and it's pretty hard riding your small bike. Think about what you really need."

"Well, I suppose I could get the same kind of bike David has. It's an okay bike. But it still costs more than $70."

"How much do you have saved?"

"About $35, plus the money Grams just sent."

"That's about $45. Would your $45 and my $70 be enough to get a bike like David's?"

"Yes. But then I'll have spent my money and it's not even for the bike I wish I had."

"That's true. Your option would be to wait until you save enough to buy the Z999999."

"It's a Z189754, Dad, and that could take months."

"So what are you going to do?"

This conversation isn't typical of most child/parent interactions. This father took the time to help his son work through the variety of needs he had and then come to his own conclusion. In a perfect world, we'd all be this patient all the time. Sometimes we can't take the debate, so we respond with, "I just said no, and that's all there is to it." Unfortunately there is no lesson in that, and the child walks away feeling totally out of control of his life.

Understanding different types of needs, and helping children to understand them, isn't easy the first time out. But with practice it gets easier. And when you practise with your children, they'll begin to internalize the conversations so that they are making their buying decisions based on their understanding of their true buying motivation.

MONEY LESSON

(AGE 10+)

From time to time, when your child indicates a need to buy something, help her to determine whether her need is based on a want, concern, problem or desire. While you won't necessarily respond to the need by coughing up the money requested, each opportunity to discuss your child's buying motivation will bring her one step closer to being able to make sound buying decisions for herself.

The more you do this, the easier it will get. It doesn't have to be done for every stated need, but it should be part of your discussion about buying big-ticket items or items in excess.

If your kid stymies you in one of these conversations, don't give up. Children have a remarkable ability to come up with the most unusual responses. Just smile. Think of it as a learning opportunity. You'll be better prepared for the next conversation.

The only way for children to gain an appreciation of what things cost and the fact that money doesn't grow on trees is to teach them.

MONEY LESSON

(AGE 12+)

The object of this lesson is to show your child how much of the money you make is spent on maintaining the family: housing, clothing, food, telephone bill, electricity and everything else, and how much is left at the end of the month. You want to show that money is finite. Since kids take many maintenance items for granted (kids don't think about the electricity bill, so they don't remember to turn off the lights when they leave the room), this lesson will be important in adjusting their perceptions.

If you already have a written budget, you can use it in teaching this lesson. If you don't, consider making one. Also gather together copies of the household bills so you can show what each item costs. Save a few of your weekly grocery receipts (and any other receipts for typical expenditures for which you have no bills) for this exercise.

1. Ask your child to list all the things he thinks you have to pay for each month. Next, ask him to estimate how much each of those things cost.

2. Ask your child to estimate how much you earn each month. Ask him to estimate how much you have left over once you have paid all the normal household bills.

3. Tell your child how much you make. The likelihood is he will have greatly underestimated how much you make and will see you as being very rich. Write your monthly income amount down on a piece of paper.

4. Now, review your child's list of things you have to pay. First, add the things (using your budget as a guide) that were left off the list. In adding these items, help to direct your child to the expense before you add it to the list. "Malcolm, you like to watch television. Do you think we have to pay to get those shows on our TV?"

5. As you add each new item, show your child the bill so he can get an idea of what it costs. This will help to pave the way for step 6.

6. Ask your child to review the items he put on the list to see if he wants to adjust any of the dollar amounts. Having just completed step 5, he may want to. "Well, Malcolm, if it costs $40 a month for the television cable, do you think it only costs $25 a month for our electricity bill?" Once he has adjusted his figures (only if he has felt he should), you can then show him the actual bill.

7. Total up what it costs to pay all the household bills. Don't forget to include the amount of income tax you pay. Write that figure under the income figure you wrote down earlier. Subtract the expense figure and show the total amount of money remaining when all your family's expenses have been paid.

8. Now it's time to hold a discussion about expenses you pay less regularly, but for which you must budget — such as prescriptions, dental bills, movies and other entertainment, holidays, furniture, car repairs, etc.

9. You may also want to reinforce the importance of putting aside money to help those less fortunate.

While children seven to nine may find the detail in this exercise a little tedious, you can still use a version of it to bring home the main points. For example, when you go grocery shopping, tell your child how much you have to spend. As you do your shopping, keep a running total of how much you've spent. "Okay, Molly, so far we've spent $30 and we're adding a box of detergent that costs $4. So now we've spent $34."

Remember, your objective is to demonstrate that money is exhaustible, and when it runs out, that's it!

THE CONCEPT OF RELATIVE VALUE

An important lesson in becoming a good consumer revolves around the idea of relative value. I've heard lots of parents talk about how little appreciation their children show for their clothes, toys or special treats. One mother lamented that her children were downright ingrates. In many cases, disparaging children for their lack of values isn't really fair since they have no appreciation for what it takes to meet their voracious consumer appetites. A lesson in relative value can make all the difference.

Relative value refers to the relationship between what an item costs and what you have to do to pay for it. For example, what does it cost to take your child to a concert? Now, relate that to how long your child would have to save her allowance to be able to buy the concert ticket. If it costs $40 for the ticket and your daughter gets $5 a week in pocket money, she would have to save her entire allowance for eight weeks to be able to afford the concert ticket. For eight weeks, that would mean no movies, no magazines, no nothing. That can put a whole new perspective on the real cost of that ticket.

Once your kids are comfortable with the concept of relative value, find ways to use the concept to bring the lesson home. If your child has a job, you can talk about relative value in terms of how many papers have to be delivered, how many lawns have to be cut or how many baby-sitting jobs have to be done relative to the purchase of an item. For example, if your child wants to buy an expensive new bicycle, expressing the cost of that bike in terms of the work that must be completed first will bring home the true cost of the bike. And by sharing the cost of special purchases, you will reinforce the concept of relative value.

Since not all purchases will be shared or made based on your child's "income," relating the cost of an item to how long you have to work will also reinforce the relative value. For example, if you plan to take a holiday, talk about what that holiday costs in terms of how long you will have to work to pay for it.

MONEY LESSON
(AGE 12+)

Tell your child how much money you make per hour; even if you are not paid by the hour, work it out. Deduct your total expenses (including income tax) from this hourly wage to show your remaining disposable income per hour.

Now it's time to go shopping. Tell your child to pretend she has your hourly disposable income to spend on a new car. Ask your child to choose a car she would like to drive and write down the price of that car. (You can make this as simple as a look through the car ads in the newspaper, or as detailed as a visit to one or two car dealerships.) Divide the car's price by the hourly disposable income amount to show how many hours your child would have to work to buy the car. Ask your child if she would be prepared to work that many hours for that specific car. If she chose a less expensive car, how many hours would she have to work?

Repeat the exercise with a holiday purchase, the purchase of a piece of furniture and a personal computer.

Teaching relative value shouldn't be arduous. Resist the urge to make every purchase into an lesson. Many opportunities will naturally arise when you can reinforce the concept of relative value. The lesson shouldn't seem like a lesson, for rest assured that if it does, or if it seems as if they've heard it before, your kids just won't give it their attention.

MONEY LESSON

(AGE 12+)

The object of this lesson is to show your child how incomes vary and how people live differently based on the amount of money they have at their disposal.

Gather together the employment pages of your local newspaper and ask your child to choose four or five jobs listed. Guide your child to choose different types of positions — office administrator, computer, service (waitress, cashier), trade (plumber, electrician), middle and senior management. You may also wish to include professionals (doctors, lawyers) or self-employed (writers, beauty-salon owners) on this list to widen your child's perspective.

Have your child create an identity for the people who might do these jobs, giving them each a name and describing what each person is like: What does she do for fun? Does he have a family? Does she like music, movies, gardening?

For example, the doctor's name is Daphne. She is married with two children and loves to go bicycle riding in the summer. When referring to each person, use his or her name and occupation (e.g., Doctor Daphne, Writer Bill, Nurse David, Computer Chris.)

If the income is stated in the ad, your job will be easier. If no income is stated, you will have to help your child make a telephone call to find out approximately how much the position pays. For professional and self-employed positions, suggest that your child survey friends and family members to see the amount of income this type of employment generates.

Tell your child that people typically spend 30–35 percent of their income on housing. Let your child figure out (or you can do the actual calculation for younger children) how much, in dollars, that would be for each of the jobs itemized. (For the purposes of this exercise, assume each family, if there is a family, has a sole income provider.)

Now, back to the newspapers. Look at the rental property advertisements and ask your child where each of those people could live based on their income. Reinforce that each individual's personal circumstances will have to be taken into account in deciding where to live. For example, since Doctor Daphne has a husband and two children, would a one-bedroom apartment really work well for them? How difficult would it be for Nurse David to live far from his job (for less expensive accommodations) and commute if he has to work shifts? Will the fact that Computer Chris has children affect where he chooses to live?

You can also do this exercise with the view to discussing what type of property each could afford to buy (assuming the down payment is already saved) in terms of carrying costs. You will have to explain what a mortgage is (see chapter 12) and how mortgage payments are determined so you can come up with a monthly mortgage cost.

DISCUSSION POINTS
How does each person's housing needs differ based on family circumstances? Since Writer Bill lives by himself, is it easier for him to find accommodation than it is for Doctor Daphne, who has a family?

What would happen if any of these people lost their jobs or got sick and couldn't work? (So you child doesn't quietly worry about his safety if the unforeseen should happen, tell him that there are things people can do to help protect themselves. Tell him what your family does to protect itself.)

What should our society do to help people who have experienced a setback financially and who can no longer provide for their families?

What should extended families do to help members who are facing financial uncertainty through no fault of their own?

What is the impact on families and societies when family (direct and extended) and society do not help people who are in need?

What is the impact on individuals who do not take their financial responsibilities seriously?

MONEY ISN'T EVERYTHING

Much of the discussion in this chapter has focused on the value of money and the important role it plays in life. But a lesson on money and value would be incomplete without addressing the fact that money is not the be-all and end-all of life. Money has its place. It is a useful tool in getting the things we need. However, if we don't want it to become an all-consuming obsession, we have to put it in perspective.

How your children view money will be a reflection of your personal views of money. If you are always harping on how little you have and what you can't afford, your kids will get the message that money is mean and not having enough of it makes life miserable. If you constantly worry aloud about money, your children will come to see money as a problem, instead of a tool. I don't mean to say you should spin an imaginary world of total financial bliss for your children. That's not realistic and will certainly not prepare them for the real world. It's all a matter of balance.

There are lots of happy events that can reinforce the fact that money isn't everything. A picnic lunch in the park is more delicious than lunch in the kitchen and cost no more. A walk through a park talking about the trees, the flowers and the neighbourhood dogs is as compelling for a young child as a visit to the zoo. A movie seen at a discount is no less satisfying than a movie at full price.

For children to learn to live with and without money, they need to see that it doesn't have to be the centre point of their lives. It's a tool. It helps you buy a new bike. But you can buy a second-hand bike and work together to fix it up and accomplish the same objective.

As an avid garage sale shopper — I call it "going garage sailing" — I am often surprised at the reaction of my peers. My enthusiasm simply isn't shared by a lot of people. That's not because of the time it takes, but because those goods are *used*. "I could never put my baby in some other child's clothes," one friend said.

The importance placed on the labels, those inside as well as those worn worn as insignia, is a new construct of our society. When I was in school, everyone wore a uniform. Most of us hated it. But there was no debate in the morning about what we were going to wear to school. No one was labelled a geek for what he or she wore. It was one less peer pressure we had to deal with. The pressure to conform seems to come earlier and earlier for children. Your attitude and approach to dealing with money and value will either reinforce or help to mitigate your children's need to bow to this pressure.

It takes a lot of effort to learn about money and value. Cut your kid some slack. We all indulge ourselves from time to time. Be as kind to your child as you are to yourself. In teaching our children about money and value, we want them to feel good about money and about themselves in relation to money. We want to help them to see it as one of the tools of living and not as an end in itself. We want to help them understand that they can't buy everything they want, that a purchase today has a cost in terms of future satisfaction, that they need to choose, and that the decision is theirs.

4 ALL ABOUT ALLOWANCES

Before children can learn to manage money well, they first need to be able to get their hands on the stuff. The debate about allowance — how much children should receive and who should manage it — rages. Some people feel an allowance should have no strings attached. Others think it should be tied to chores in the home, school grades or behaviour ("If you don't smarten up, I'll cut off your allowance!"). When it comes to whether children should or should not have jobs, some parents feel school is a child's job, and any other work detracts from potential success at school. Others think that a part-time job is perfectly fine, while still others believe that a part-time job is essential because it begins the development of a good work ethic.

At a dinner gathering one night, I was asked what the topic of my next book would be. When I told the gentleman inquiring, he asked me my opinion on allowances. I told him. He just about climbed across the dinner table as he roared at me. As far as he was concerned, children should have everything they ask for. And there should be no expectations with regard to their handling of money. Real life was hard and it would come soon enough. When I asked him how children would develop the skills for real life, he blustered, shrugged and said that it would come in time, once they were on their own.

Now, if you had the choice of learning to walk a tightrope with or without a safety net, which would you choose? Learning about money at a young age, when mistakes can be easily remedied or do not have a long-lasting impact, makes a lot more sense than learning about money when you also have to pay the rent, meet your loan commitments and all the rest. Because many people didn't have the opportunity to practise with a safety net, they fall and hurt themselves, sometimes seriously.

The strings attached to the money you received as a child will have a strong bearing on the strings you attach to your children's money. Perhaps you were never given an allowance and had to work for every penny you got. This may colour the way you look at allowances in general. Your allowance may have been tied to chores, or you may have been required to save all the money received as gifts.

Whatever your own personal experience with money as a child, try to put them aside as you read through this chapter. After all, just because you had to walk seven miles to school in blinding snow with a hole in your shoe doesn't mean you necessarily want the same thing for your own children.

When you begin to think about an allowance for your kids, there some questions you need to ask yourself:

- Should I give my child an allowance?
- At what age should I start an allowance?
- Should an allowance be tied to anything in particular?
- What do I expect of my child in terms of how that allowance is managed?
- How much should my child get as an allowance?
- How often should my child receive an allowance?
- What will the allowance be used for?
- Am I prepared to give advances, loans and extra money, and if so, will there be any strings attached?
- How will I help my child learn money management?

IS AN ALLOWANCE APPROPRIATE?

The simplest way to start children off on the road to sound financial well-being is to give them some loot to manage. How much you give will depend on your personal circumstances and your attitude towards the whole concept of an allowance.

The alternative to an allowance, and a trap for most parents, is the dole system. That's when your kid asks for some cash and you dole it out. Since the dole system has no limit, there is no reason for a child to make a decision on relative value. In fact, if you ask a child on the dole system if he wants an allowance, ten to one he will choose to remain on the much more lucrative system he has. After all, while he will have to put up with some lecturing and lamenting from his parents, he'll likely get just about anything he wants.

Another downside to the dole system is that you remove all control from your child. You get to decide which of his requests are valid enough for consideration, and your child feels like a beggar. Your child learns the gimme's really well and you grow resentful of the constant requests for cash.

48

"But Mom, I only need two dollars." "Gee Dad, it only costs five dollars." "Can I have another quarter? Another dollar?"

If you're currently on the dole system and don't fully appreciate what it's costing you, consider keeping track of all the small change you hand over to your kid in a month. You may be surprised at how large his allowance is!

To learn how to manage money responsibly, children need an income they can rely on — one given at regular intervals. The experience of handling a steady flow of cash will teach many fundamental skills, including how to manage a cash flow, how to plan ahead, the skill of setting goals (both short- and long-term) and how to save to satisfy a goal. With your guidance, this cash flow can also be used to teach important lessons in borrowing and lending, the pleasure derived from generosity, how to be a good consumer and the importance of considering those less fortunate.

Ultimately your children will learn all about the family's budget and how they can contribute to the family's financial well-being: ways to save expenses (turn off those darned lights!) and how to shop smartly (who better to advise on the purchase of the family's home computer than your techno-whiz?). They will learn that the little things add up (20 percent saved on this item means two dollars that can be spent on something else) and that every nickel does count. Children progress pretty quickly from bubblegum to Guess jeans. While the dollar amounts they spend rise dramatically as they age, their respect for money doesn't automatically increase proportionately. Only by helping them to learn the important money lessons will they develop the appropriate attitudes towards money.

AT WHAT AGE SHOULD I START AN ALLOWANCE?

Most child-development experts say that children are ready to deal with the concept of handling an allowance at about age five. While children may understand that money is used to buy things at an earlier age — usually at about three — they can't conceptually understand what an allowance is or how it should be used and managed.

Children younger than five can still be initiated into the world of money. Giving a child the appropriate change to pay for an item in a store can begin the process. So, too, can letting your child put coins in the newspaper box in exchange for a paper. Both these activities help to teach children that money is exchanged for other things and that once the money is given in exchange, it's gone — finis, finito, bye-bye.

Since you need to start somewhere, and earlier is better than later, you may wish to start your three-year old off with an allowance of 25 cents a week. This is enough for your child to make small purchases of her own.

At age five, your child can begin to conceptualize the purpose of an allowance — she now has her own money and has to plan in order to buy some of the things she wants. She will also begin to learn about relative value as she begins to make decisions — with your help — about whether or not to buy a specific item. If your kid is older than five and you haven't yet started her on an allowance, now's the time.

In giving an allowance, a neat idea is to ask your child how she would like to receive the money. Let's say, for example, that your daughter receives two dollars a week in pocket money. Does she want it in bills, in quarters, in dimes or nickels? While this may not seem like a significant point to you, your child may find that receiving her money in bills makes it hard to implement her budgeting plan. On the other hand, if she gets eight quarters, she may find it easier to set aside the money for the various parts of her budget: saving, spending and sharing.

SHOULD AN ALLOWANCE BE TIED TO ANYTHING IN PARTICULAR?

First of all, think about why you're starting your child on an allowance. Is it to teach him that you work hard for your money? Is it to reward him for good behaviour or good grades? Is it to pay him for doing chores? Or is it provide him with a tool to learn about money management?

The objective of providing your child with an allowance should be to teach him money-management skills. The fact that you work hard for your money will be brought home when your child learns relative value. Money doesn't work as a reward for good behaviour. Good behaviour is based on an understanding of right and wrong, thoughtfulness, caring and consideration, along with myriad other positive attributes, all of which have to be internalized. Good grades are your child's *responsibility*. School is his primary job, and good grades are an indication that he is doing his job well. If you provide financial reward for good grades, you are externalizing the reward. Instead, the reward should be internalized: the self-esteem and pride that accompanies having done well.

As for an allowance being payment for chores, who pays you to do the chores in your home? Chores are a part of each individual's responsibility to the family. Payment for regular chores negates a child's individual responsibility as a member of the family unit. (Payment for extra household tasks — those above and beyond a child's normal chores — is fine when they are specifically doing the task to earn some money. More on this later.)

If you're concerned about ensuring that your child knows his effort in completing chores is recognized, using reinforcement other than a monetary reward will create a more balanced outcome. Make sure each member of the family knows how important his or her contribution is to the whole family. "Peter, when you clean the litter box twice each day, you make the whole house nicer to live in. We don't have any nasty smells, the cats can use a clean box, instead of pooping just anywhere, and both Dad and I don't have to add that to our list of chores." When assigning a chore, make sure it is a job that has real value. Make-work is easy to spot, and if your child is expected to believe that his commitment is important, the job has to be important too. Finally, if your kid doesn't do the job, don't do it for him. And don't threaten to withhold his allowance. Remember, the allowance is separate from the responsibility of completing his chores. A little encouragement and a gentle reminder will slowly bring the lesson home. Be patient and trust that over time he'll need fewer reminders.

HOW SHOULD I EXPECT MY CHILD TO MANAGE HER ALLOWANCE?

One of the most difficult parts of allowance-giving for most parents is establishing expectations for how that allowance will be managed. Does a child have the right to spend all her allowance on anything she wants every week? Actually, while it's her money, the liberty to spend at will does nothing to teach good money management. In fact, it isn't a liberty afforded to us as adults. Since we are required to spend a certain amount of our hard-earned money in fixed expenses, regardless of what we want to buy ourselves — we have to keep a roof over our head and our children fed — allowing kids to do as they will with their entire allowance isn't a true representation of money management in the real world.

In learning how to manage money, children need to see that there are a variety of purposes for money (not just the immediate gratification of spending it). Spending is a part of the equation, but so, too, is saving and sharing with others less fortunate.

Look at an allowance as having three components: (1) the part to be saved, (2) the part to be shared, and (3) the part to be spent. This third part of the allowance equation can itself be broken down into two parts: the spending kids want to be able to do on a whim (their mad money), and the spending they intend to do based on specific expenses and expressly stated goals (their planned spending). Spending on a whim comes naturally to most people. Saving, sharing and planned spending are all ideas that have to be introduced, practised and reinforced.

One way to clearly differentiate between the different purposes for money is to set up money holders for each purpose. For example, you can use four containers, clearly labelled: Savings, Sharing, Mad Money, Planned Spending.

The rule of thumb for saving is that you should save ten percent of your income. If your child gets five dollars a week, the first thing to reinforce is that 50 cents needs to be put in the Savings container. The rule of thumb for sharing is that you should put aside five to ten percent for charity, so into the Sharing container should go 25 to 50 cents.

Now comes the hard part. What percentage of the remaining money should be planned spending versus mad money? That depends on whether your child is expected to pay specific costs for herself, and what long-term spending goals she has. Let's say, for example, that as part of her allowance you provide your child with enough money to pay for her bus fare to and from school each week. That money should be set aside in the Planned Spending container to be used each day as needed. Let's also say that you expect your child to buy gifts for special occasions from her allowance. Together, you'll have to figure out how many gifts are bought each year, and what percentage of her allowance needs to be set aside each week so the money will be there when the special occasion rolls around. Your child might also have a special purchase in mind. Let's say she wants to buy herself a new Walkman. You can help her determine how much she needs to put aside each week so that dream can become a reality.

The rest of the money is mad money. She can spend it, she can put it towards her long-term savings goal (the Walkman), she can do anything she wants with it!

HOW MUCH ALLOWANCE SHOULD MY CHILD GET?

The amount you choose to give your child will depend on how much you can afford, your child's age, and what you expect your child to do with her allowance. If, for example, the most you can afford is five dollars a week, so be it. That's a good way to start learning about money management. Naturally, younger children need, and are capable of handling, less money. If all your child is buying is candy and the occasional toy, you may want to start her off with a relatively small sum. At five years old, 50 cents a week may be more than sufficient. Some people use the age of their child as a guide; a five-year old gets five dollars, a seven-year old gets seven dollars. You're the best judge of the amount that will be most appropriate for your child. Just remember that it needs to be enough so that your child can save, share and spend (mad money and planned spending included).

Children who are old enough to set goals and budget need more so they have something to work with. While many parents are stuck on the two-dollar-a-week allowance, just think about what two dollars can buy now and you'll have a good idea of how effective that amount will be in teaching money management. If you got an allowance as a child, why don't you try using the inflation table on page 141 to see just how much your child will need today to have the same buying power? You'll be very surprised!

Once again, if you expect older children — 13 and up — to buy some of their own clothes, pay for their own haircuts and plan for big-ticket buys such as camp, a television or car insurance, you'll have to figure out what each of those things costs. To those routine (and budgetable) costs you'll need to add some mad money, some money for establishing a regular savings habit and some money for charity.

As your child grows older, you need to periodically review and adjust the amount he receives. It's a good idea to pick a specific time of year — the beginning of the year, your child's birthday week, the beginning of a new school year — and make the review routine. Keep in mind, too, that as your child grows, he should become responsible for generating some income of his own. At 12, your kid is old enough to start earning some of his own money.

In figuring out how much to give as an allowance, ask your child to list the five most important things he wants to do with his money. If he is an avid reader and wishes to buy his own books, he'll need more than a child who is only interested in candy. Listen carefully to what your youngster has to say.

If your son is looking for a hefty increase, ask him to give you a written proposal or a formal presentation explaining how much he wants and why. If you were asking for a raise at work, you'd have to justify your request. Perhaps he feels it is time he started buying his own clothes. You can negotiate the initial amount and attached responsibilities, and implement the plan slowly. Moving from no clothing allowance to a year's clothing allowance in one fell swoop is a recipe for disaster. Let your child assume responsibility in small increments.

Before you do your allowance review, take some time to think about what you want to accomplish over the next year in teaching your child about money. You and your spouse should talk about how much responsibility you feel your child can now take on. Perhaps you wish to start your son on an investment program. If so, you'll need to do a fair amount of teaching, and you'll need to up his allowance to take the money for investing into account. You'll also have to carefully monitor his progress to ensure the funds are being directed to the appropriate new category in his budget.

HOW OFTEN SHOULD MY CHILD RECEIVE AN ALLOWANCE?

Younger children will find it easier to handle their money if they are given a small amount every week. Consider what time of week is best. If your experience says that giving an allowance at the beginning of the weekend means it's all gone by Monday, then give it on Monday or Wednesday. While you want your child to accept responsibility, young children need some help in developing the skills. The timing of the allowance may make all the difference. Children who are older and have established many of the habits of budgeting should be asked when and how often they prefer to receive their allowance. While some kids like getting a little money each week, others may prefer a lump sum once a month, allowing them to plan spending for the month.

Whatever allowance schedule you establish with your children, make sure you stick to it. It's demeaning for anyone to have to constantly ask for money. And providing the allowance on time will send a subtle message about the value of honoring commitments.

WHAT WILL THE ALLOWANCE BE USED FOR?

When we look at how much money is appropriate as an allowance, we must factor in things we expect our kids to manage themselves. While a seven-year-old may only be able to manage the budgeting of her weekly bus fare, a 15-year-old is more than capable of handling a budget that includes the purchase of personal hygiene products, clothing and school supplies.

What do you do if your daughter takes her monthly clothing allotment and blows it all on a dress for a party? So be it. The money is gone.

You can't stand seeing her in those ratty old jeans. That's your problem, not hers. At some point you have to allow your children to be self-determining. If you object to your daughter showing up to special family gatherings wearing something you consider totally inappropriate, you can ask her to be considerate of your feelings and dress a little more conservatively. Take her shopping for a special outfit and set it aside for those occasions.

You can't stand to see your hard-earned money being spent on the trashy clothes she buys. It's not your money. It's her money. You gave it to her and it's hers to manage. Let her live with the consequences of her purchase decisions. If she comes to you and says, "Mom, I don't have anything to wear! I need a decent dress," resist the urge to take her on a shopping spree out of sheer relief. If there's no consequence to her purchase decisions — if she hasn't considered the relative value of her purchases — she needs to experience the natural consequence. Your best response would be, "Molly, I'm sorry you don't think you have anything decent to wear. Maybe you should budget for some new clothes out of your next allowance."

Clothing is often a point of disagreement between parents and children. But there are hundreds of other examples. Your son may arrive home one day with a haphazard haircut that makes him look, at least from your perspective, like a barbarian. Grit your teeth and smile. Your daughter may decide to spend her long-saved planned spending money on something other than her original goal. That's her choice. Your son arrives home with a beat-up car on its last legs. And he paid *what* for it? You can say, "Get rid of that thing — you're not parking it in front of my house!" or you can say, "Have you considered what it will cost to find a parking place for that?"

The way you react to your children's purchase decision will affect the ways they continue to make their decisions. In a perfect world your child would have your exquisite taste, would ask for your advice on each purchase decision and would demonstrate a healthy helping of common sense in all things financial. But it's not a perfect world, and making mistakes is part of the whole process.

When your children make mistakes, you can do a couple of things. You can rant and rave, which will win you no points as a balanced and open-minded parent. You can rush in and bail your kid out, which will do nothing in terms of teaching what may be a very important lesson in consequences. Or you can help your child to determine how he will fix the problem. If your daughter dents the car, she should not only have to pay for the repair, she should also have to take time from *her* busy schedule to have the repairs done. If your son spends $200 on a pair of running shoes (when a $50 pair would have been fine), he should have to go without whatever else that money was destined for: a school trip, a special purchase or his next month's supply of razors.

ADVANCES, LOANS AND EXTRA MONEY

Should you give an advance against allowances? Maybe. Should you lend money to your child? Maybe. Should you provide extra money above the normal allowance amount? Maybe. Doesn't sound very definitive, does it? It's not. Whether you decide to do any of these will be a matter of personal choice. Since life isn't black and white, there is no straightforward answer to these questions. However there are some things you should think about when making the decision.

First, each occasion will warrant consideration on its own merit. In determining whether a loan or advance is appropriate, consider the following:

- **How often does your child ask for a loan or an advance?**
Repeated requests may indicate that your child has difficulty learning how to budget and how to plan for the future. Adults manifest the same lack of skill when, rather than saving for an item, they apply for a loan. They are more comfortable with the idea of working regular repayments into their budgets than with the concept of saving a similar amount each month for a future purchase. Or their need for immediate gratification outweighs their patience in implementing a planned spending approach. However the cost of this borrow-spend-repay strategy is very high. Every cent in interest paid on a loan (including on a credit-card balance) is money wasted. It's money that could be used to increase savings or provide for other needs. It's money down the tubes. So, do you want your child to become a borrower or to be skilled at planned spending?

If your kid doesn't ask for a loan or advance with any regularity — if it really is a case of an emergency or a special occasion — then using it as a lesson in how to borrow, and the costs associated, can be very worthwhile. (There is more on how to teach children about credit in chapter 12)

- **How often does your child ask for extra money?**
Ditto. Everything said in the previous point applies here.
Keep in mind that while we all must learn to live within our means, there will be times when you will want to help your child by offering some extra money. Let's say, for example, that an opportunity arises for your child to go on a short holiday with some chums from school. You may decide it's worthwhile to offer up the needed funds to make it happen. That's your choice. But once you've given the money, you need to remember that it was a gift. If you give it without strings, then you can't use it as a point of guilt ("Remember when I shelled out that extra $400 for that trip to Washington?") and you can't use it as a threat ("If you don't toe the line, you'll never see another penny from me.")

- **If you extend a loan or give an allowance advance, what is your expectation for repayment?**
  If you go to a bank to borrow money, your banker has an expectation that the money will be repaid. He will expect the repayment of the principal borrowed, in full, with interest, and on time based on the repayment schedule established. If you want your child to learn about borrowing, you need to set your own expectations.

- **What will you do if your child resorts to begging?**
  If you haven't experienced this, you're very lucky! At least once in each child's life she will resort to begging. She may plead. She may whine. She may cry. She will simply work on you till she wears you down. If she succeeds, you're doomed. While it may not be a conscious decision, you are making a decision; and it is a decision that positively reinforces a very negative strategy and teaches your child that simply having more patience than you lets her win.

The best deterrent to the begging syndrome is to establish a set of ground rules about money, shopping, loans and advances in a discussion with your child, or at the very least the very first time the little beggar starts her routine. Children need rules to understand how the game is played. Your rules should emphasize the value of planning ahead, patience, respect for others, self-discipline and self-respect. For example, you might tell your child the following:

- You receive an allowance. If you need more money, we can talk about it and look at ways you can earn it (extra work around the house, getting a job).

- When we go shopping, don't automatically expect to be given a treat. If you want to buy something specific, you have the option of taking a shopping list and the appropriate amount of money. If you see something you really want to buy while you're out, either have the money available to pay for it or plan to return to the store to buy it. Don't expect to receive a loan or an advance on the spot. Every credit application takes time, and on-the-spot loans aren't a part of the way our family operates.

- If you think begging may work, think again. Begging, crying, whining and pouting (or any other behaviour that makes the shopping experience unpleasant) will have the immediate result of making me angry. The long-term result may be that you will not be invited on future shopping trips.

- Everyone in our family lives on a budget. If you need something you must plan for it. If you see something you really need or is a very good value, you can ask if it fits into the budget. If it does, you *may* get it. If it doesn't — if I say, "We don't have any money in our budget for that today" — give it up and be prepared to return with your own money to make the purchase.

Make your expectations clear by establishing the rules up front. Making up the rules as you go isn't fair to children. And it doesn't teach them much other than that you are the ultimate provider and your reaction will be based on how you feel that day. If your children know the rules, they are much more likely to follow them. Be assured they will test every limit you set. Also know that by sticking to the rules you will be sending a clear message about what is appropriate and how you expect your child to behave.

HOW WILL I HELP MY CHILD LEARN MONEY MANAGEMENT?

Think back to the effort, patience and time it took to potty-train your beautiful toddler. Remember the effort, patience and time it took to teach your child how to ride a bicycle, skate or swim. Money management is the term for a whole bunch of individual skills wrapped up in one neat package. But each of the skills needs to be taught, practised and reinforced. And each takes time to acquire.

You have the most influence in terms of teaching your kids about money. After parents, in rank order, teachers, personal experience, books or magazines, television, friends and siblings are the sources for money information. Since what you do and say will have the most impact on your children, you have to be sure you say what you mean and you mean what you say. An honest, straightforward approach to explaining money matters works best. Don't take the easy way out. "I don't have the money to buy you that thingamajig" as a pat answer for each request you don't want to fulfill teaches little. Instead, use each opportunity to teach the important lessons of budgeting, relative value and patience.

By the time your children go to school, they will have already learned a lot from you about money. Even if you choose not to take an active role in teaching your children about money, they will learn most of what they take into their future lives from what you *do* (as opposed to what you *say*). If you save regularly, they will see savings as an important part of money management. If you are an avid investor, they will develop an interest in investing. If you regularly donate to charity, your children will likely follow your example.

They will know whether you are an impulse shopper or a planned spender, whether you are generous or miserly with your money, whether you see money as a tool or as a god. If you comparison shop, they will learn from you. If you place a strong value on expensive brands, they will hear your message.

I knew a couple who were distinct opposites when it came to money. The father was a generous spirit who impulse bought and loved to satisfy his children's every wish. The mother was a tightwad, begrudging most spending. The father's attitude was, "Money is a tool for making our lives more comfortable." The mother's attitude was, "We don't have enough money." The father gave his children money to buy gifts for loved ones. The mother expected her children to fund their gift-giving themselves.

The messages this couple's children received were very mixed. While that's pretty usual for many families, it doesn't help to promote learning, since inconsistent messages are confusing for children. If you are teaching your children about money as a couple, it's important you develop a joint plan about what you will teach.

Differences in style are natural. How you demonstrate those differences to your kids will have an impact on the lessons they eventually put to use in their own lives. Talk about how you want to teach your children the important money lessons. Starting from a shared belief — even if only in the basic ground rules — will go a long way to delivering a consistent message to your children.

5 MAKING MONEY

At some point, your child's need for money will outstrip what you're prepared to fork out. It may come sooner or it may come later, but it will come. And when it does, it's time to introduce the concept of working for money. It's a simple equation. It's a matter of your child exchanging his time and effort for your, or someone else's, money. If your child already has a handle on the concept of relative value, he already knows that money is given in exchange for work, and that when you buy an item you can calculate the cost in terms of the amount of work that had to be done to buy that item.

Depending on your child's age, you may have to help him by providing paid-for-work around the home. Create a list of tasks that need to be done around the house and assign a dollar value to each. Some tasks can be one-time jobs, like raking the fall leaves, while others can be regularly scheduled jobs that are done in addition to your child's chores for a regular pay, such as cleaning the kitty litter. Assign a date to each job so there is a sense of timeliness to the work, and take care to remove jobs that have been completed and add new jobs as they need to be done.

Ask your child for ideas of things she can do around the house. You may find yourself with a wonderful little worker who loves to weed. I hate weeding and will pay well to have someone do it for me. If my kid wants the job of weeding, she can have it.

You can post your list on the fridge or corkboard. As your child needs money, he can choose an item from the list and complete the task. To keep the whole process businesslike, you may want to establish a contract that states what the job is, when it will be completed and how much it will pay. Both you and your child should sign the contract. When the contract is fulfilled, pay your child.

Here are two golden rules about paying for work:

- Never pay until the job is completed. You wouldn't buy a half-baked cake or a half-sewn dress, so don't pay for a half-cleaned garage.

- Pay immediately when the job is done. Make sure you have the money on hand and shell it out as soon as the work contract has been fulfilled.

When we break the first golden rule, it is usually because we feel sorry for our kids. But we shouldn't. A deal is a deal. Perhaps we figure they're never going to finish the job; we might as well pay them and get them out of our hair so we can finish up. That doesn't teach anything positive about work ethic and responsibility. Stick to your original plan. If your kid doesn't finish the job, she doesn't get paid. If it takes her all day, so be it. It is your child's choice to spend that amount of time on the task.

While I try to live by these golden rules, I have also bent the rules a little myself. When Amanda needed extra money last December for her holiday shopping, we worked out an arrangement where she would do some scanning of artwork on my computer in exchange for a predetermined hourly wage. She was about halfway through the job when she needed to finish her shopping, so I asked her if she wanted an advance on the rest of the job. "No," she said, "if you pay me first I may not finish the job. Just pay me up till now and I'll earn the rest before I go back to school." Pretty neat, huh? Not my doing, I have to admit, but it's pretty neat anyway. Amanda just happens to know herself really well and is pretty honest about her motivations.

You need to help your children develop that understanding of themselves. Not everyone loves cleaning out the garage. But if the pay is right and the need is strong enough, you may still be able to get your garage cleaned up while your son earns the extra pocket money he needs to be able to afford those concert tickets to see Smashing Pumpkins.

When we break the second rule it's because we just didn't plan ahead. But it can be very demotivating for a worker to get to the end of a hard job and have only a promise of payment to show for it. If you expect your kid to stick to his end of the bargain and do the job right, you need to meet your commitments by having the money available for payment when the job is completed.

MONEY LESSON
(AGE 10+)

Children should be encouraged to think of different things they can do to earn money. Often they need to be prompted to generate ideas, and a game is the best way to make the whole process fun. This game also teaches an important brainstorming skill called mind-mapping. (On the following page is an example of a mind-map you can use as a guide.)

Get a big piece of paper — consider using a sheet of construction paper or brown paper wrap — that covers the tabletop or a big space on the floor. You'll also need some coloured markers to make your mind-map interesting and to differentiate between ideas.

Begin by explaining that there are three ways to make money:

- Manufacturing — by making something someone else will want to buy

- Retailing — by selling something someone else has made

- Service — by providing a service for a fee.

Using a blue marker, write the word "jobs" in the middle of the paper. Off to each side, write the words "manufacturing," "retailing" and "service."

First ask your child to give you examples of things that are manufactured. As she responds, use a red marker to write her ideas in a box on the mind-map beside the word "manufacturing." Now ask her for a list of retail stores (by category, not store name). Write her responses beside the word "retailing." Next ask for examples of services done for a fee. Write her answers beside the word "service."

cookies, wooden toys, ceramics, other crafts, lemonade

baby-sitting, pet-sitting, running errands, snow removal

cars, newspapers, cookies, clothing, jewellery

bakery, clothing store, grocery store, bookstore, video shop

Manufacturing

Retailing

JOBS

Services

plumbing, dry cleaning, house keeping, gardening

walking the dog, weeding gardens, raking leaves, cutting grass, washing windows, washing cars, baby-sitting, pet-sitting, running errands, snow

Next, ask her for ideas of things she could manufacture and sell. With a different colour marker, write her ideas in another box on the mind-map beside the word "manufacture."

Follow the same pattern in completing the mind-map. Next, ask her for ideas of things she could retail. With yet another colour marker, write her ideas in another box on the mind-map beside the word "retailing."

Then ask for ideas of services people might pay her to do for them and write them beside the word "services."

It's amazing how ingenious kids can be when they set out to make a buck. My husband loves to tell the story of when his son, Kris, decided to earn some money. At only six, he set up a desk on the lawn with the sign DINOSAUR INFORMATION — 25¢. He carefully arranged a few plastic dinosaurs on this desk for atmosphere. One gentleman stopped by and paid to hear what Kris had to say. Five minutes later he handed Kris a dollar bill and said, "Kid, I don't have enough time to hear all you know about dinosaurs, so here's a buck."

You may have to help your child identify skills or knowledge she can use to earn some money. A good place to start might be to have her sit down and make a list of the things she can do. Perhaps your daughter can knit, in which case making sweaters or baby hats and booties may be an option. If your son is really good at painting, he may be able to get a job sprucing up rooms or staining decks and fences. Perhaps your daughter is really great with younger kids. She could hire herself out to neighbouring parents who need a couple of hours' respite on weekends.

STARTING A BUSINESS

Some children have a very strong entrepreneurial spirit. They want to work, and they love the financial rewards that go with it. Those children may be motivated to go into business for themselves so they can have a regular cash flow.

What's the difference between doing odd jobs and being in business for yourself?

The difference between doing a job and being in business for yourself relates to how consistently you work. When you work periodically, usually only in response to your need for money, we can refer to those as "odd jobs." If you are interested in working on a regular basis, and you want to be your own boss, then you have to go into business for yourself.

What are some of the things you need to know if you're going to be in business for yourself?

There's a lot involved in starting and running your own business. You have to figure out what you have that people will want to buy (what you can make, what you can sell, or services you can provide). You also have to learn cash flow management skills, determine your responsibilities to your customers, and figure out how to keep the business going over the long term.

GOING INTO BUSINESS

Many of the skills associated with being in business for yourself are basic money-management skills such as budgeting. These will be covered in other chapters of the book. In this discussion about developing a business, the focus is on what the business owner has to do to set up a business and some of the administrative details, as well as responsibilities to customers.

In speaking with your child about setting up his own business, depending on your child's age and how she learns best, you can either read the following material and use it to guide your discussion or you can suggest your child read pages 68 to 76, after which you can discuss the topics presented.

WHAT BUSINESS CAN I DO?

Everyone can do something; it's all a matter of finding customers who are willing to pay for what you do. Perhaps you can baby-sit or offer to take care of a child regularly for one hour each weekend so that child's parents get some free time of their own. Or perhaps you are very good at a particular subject in school and can offer your services as a tutor to younger children.

I heard a story recently of an eight-year-old who was really good on her computer and knew how to make maps. Over time, she developed her own small business making maps for real estate agents for their promotional flyers and open-house invitations. She was inventive, drew on a skill she had and, over time, built up her own business.

Another very entrepreneurial young lass who had established herself as a responsible baby-sitter found she had more baby-sitting jobs than she could handle, so she began hiring her friends. She would collect the money from her customers, pay the majority to her employee and keep a small amount for herself. She had the customers, her friends needed the work, and she established quite a nice little business for herself.

One way to determine what customers will pay for is to do a market survey. When you do a market survey, you ask people questions about what they like and dislike, what services and products they currently buy or would buy, and how much they would be willing to pay. Some products and services have more chance of succeeding than others. For example, if you can provide a reasonably priced regular snow-shovelling service and several people make a commitment to using your service, you can anticipate a decent income in the winter months, providing it snows. If you are good with animals and can develop a list of customers who need you to pet-sit while they work or when they travel, you're in business. If you bake great cookies and you can find enough people who want to buy your great cookies regularly, that's it, you've found your niche.

Take some time to think about the things you can do for which people might pay. Have you considered any of the following?

- Baby-sitting (or setting up a baby-sitting agency)
- Computer-based work (such as creating flyers for garage sales)
- Arranging a street sale

- Gift wrapping (especially during the Christmas season)
- Birthday-party planner or working as a clown for children's birthday parties
- Shoeshine
- Collecting and recycling pop bottles or other returnables
- Collecting and reselling used items (such as golf balls)
- Pool-cleaning service
- Snow-removal service
- Gardening and/or lawn cutting
- Fence painting
- Window cleaning
- Growing your own seedlings and selling plants in the spring
- Grocery shopping
- Library-book/video rental returner
- Dog bather
- Gift-basket maker

DEVELOPING A BUSINESS PLAN

A business plan is a plan of what your business will be like, including where it will be, what will set you apart from the competition (other people who do the same thing you plan to do), what it will cost to start, what it will cost to run, and what your expected profits will be. It helps you determine how much you will need to get your business running so you are well prepared when you try to secure financing. Securing financing is what you do when you get someone to lend you the money you need to start your business.

Let's say you're going into business as a baker. You've decided you will make cookies. Your "competitive differentiation" — what sets you apart from your competition — is that your cookies will be made with natural fruit sugars and calorie-reduced sweeteners, perfect for those who want a calorie-wise treat.

First you have to figure out how many cookies you think you can sell each week — referred to as a market projection. This will be based on how many customers you'll have to start, how many cookies each customer will want to buy and how often each customer buys.

Business Plan
Molly McGoo's Exceptionally Great Cookies

Product: Cookies and cakes

Competitive Differentiation: These cookies will be made with natural fruit sugars and calorie-reduced sweeteners, perfect for those who want a calorie-wise treat.

Market / Income Projection
of customers to start: 12
# of cookies each customer will buy: 24
How often each will buy:
    Aunty Sally . . . . weekly
    Mrs. Brown . . . . weekly
    Mom . . . . weekly
    Mrs. Indiligo . . . . weekly
    Grandma . . . . twice a month
    Aunt Denise. . . . . once a month
    Mrs. Kavo-Langley . . . . once a month
Total number of cookies each month: 600
Price of each cookie:. $0.65
Monthly projected income: $390.00

Projected Expenses
Cost of ingredients $225.00
Electricity . . . . none
Equipment rental. . . . . none
Wages. . . . . none
Advertising $10.00
Bags for the cookies (20 bags @ 10¢/ea.). $2.00
Retail location . . . . none

Net Income (projected income minus projected expenses) **$163.00**

Next you have to figure out how much it will cost to make those cookies — referred to as your projected expenses. You have to take a lot of different costs into account, including the cost of your ingredients, electricity, equipment rental (do you have to pay for the use of the stove?) and wages if you intend to have someone help you make the cookies.

Whatever business you decide to go into, you will probably need supplies, and this will very likely be your single biggest expense. If you decide to repair bicycles, you'll need tools. If you decide to go into the car-wash business, you'll need soap, buckets, sponges and cloths. If you are going to do gardening, you'll need gardening implements, bags for weeds and, perhaps, knee pads. You'll need to discuss with your parents the things you can use from home and the things you must purchase for your business.

You will also have to add the cost of marketing and selling the cookies. Typical costs include things like the cost of marketing your product, bags for the cookies you sell and a place from which to sell them.

How many different ways can you think of to market your product? You could tell everyone you know to spread the word — your family members, your friends, your guitar teacher, your doctor and your coach. You could also find a way to show off your product or service. Perhaps you would be prepared to give away free samples at neighbourhood garage sales. (Remember to include a business card or flyer so that customers who like your product will be able to get in touch with you.) Maybe you could open up a retail stand to display your goods to your neighbours. You could make posters and post them where people will see them, such as school bulletin boards, supermarkets and libraries. Of course, you need to get permission from your parents to include your telephone number and address on a poster.

You also have to figure out how much you will sell your cookies for. Figure out what the lowest price you can charge is in order to break even (cover your expenses). Begin by adding up what it costs to produce your product or provide your service. If you're baking cookies, you'll need to add up what it costs to produce your cookies — let's say you're making 60 cookies — and then divide that by 60 to see what it costs for each cookie. Then you should check around to see what cookie sellers charge for similar cookies. Now, set your cookie price so that it is high enough to make a profit, but low enough to attract lots of customers.

If you are providing a service, you may think it's more difficult to set your price. After all, while you may not have many fixed costs, you will have a lot of time invested. Setting a fee for something someone else already does may simply require that you do some market research to see what people are already paying. For example, if you're cleaning pools, you can check around to see what other pool cleaning services charge. If you plan to provide a service no one yet provides — perhaps you plan to return library books or video rentals — then your price may have to be flexible until you decide what the right price is.

One way to determine this is to decide how much you want to make an hour or a day based on how much you can accomplish in a set amount of time. Let's say, for example, you plan to cut lawns and you know you can cut a lawn every 45 minutes, and that it takes another 15 minutes to get from one job to another. The next step is to decide how much you intend to make an hour. If you want to make $7 a hour, you'll need to charge $7 for each lawn-cutting to cover your time doing the job and travelling. If you have additional costs, such as transportation, tools or other supplies, you would factor those into your price. For example, if you are using your own lawn mower, you might decide to charge $10, so you would have an additional $3 from each job to pay for your mower or to cover the costs of maintenance and repairs.

The final step is to subtract your expenses from your income to see what your project profit is. From this profit will come your own income (how much you decide to keep for yourself), along with money you must repay to the person who financed your startup. You also need to set aside a portion of this profit to cover at least part of your next month's expenses (after all, you will have to buy more flour and eggs before you can sell more cookies).

TRACKING YOUR PROFIT

While you need to do a business plan to see how much your business will make, you also need to keep track of your income and expenses to see how much profit you are making each month. Keeping up-to-date and accurate records is an important part of running your own business.

Each month, you should complete a record of income and expenses to see how well you are doing.

Record of Income and Expenses for _____

Expenses

_____	$_____
_____	$_____
_____	$_____
_____	$_____
_____	$_____
_____	$_____

Total Expenses: $_____

Income: $_____

Profit: (Income minus total expenses) $_____

OTHER BUSINESS ADMINISTRATION

There is usually quite a bit of paperwork associated with running a business. Not only do you need to prepare a business plan to see if the business is worthwhile and keep track of your profit to see how you are doing, there are some other written documents you need to be familiar with.

You may, for example, want to make a contract with each of your customers. This contract describes what you are committed to doing as part of the job and what you will be paid when the job is complete. Both you and your customer should sign the contract so you're both aware of what's involved and the expectations for the job and for payment. The contract should also be dated.

Contract

I, Molly McGoo, agree to produce and deliver 24 EXCEPTIONALLY GREAT COOKIES to Aunty Sally every Saturday morning. These cookies will be both delicious and calorie-wise.

In exchange, Aunty Sally agrees to pay me 65¢ per cookie.

_____   _____
Molly McGoo   Aunty Sally

                                         _____
                                                      Date

Sometimes you may also want to add the date when the job will be completed to the contract. If you'll be invoicing your customer, it's also a good idea to have your customer initial the completion date when the job's finished.

Most businesses formally request payment for their goods and services in writing using an invoice. An invoice states what was delivered, how much is owing and the date payment is expected. Invoices should be numbered and should always be dated and

Malcolm's Neat Garden Service
Invoice #00007

Mr. Wilson   12/6/1996
12345 Hellium Drive, Balloon City

For services rendered:

Raking leaves	$2.00
Mowing lawn	5.00
Weeding flower beds	3.00
Trimming edges	2.00
Invoice Total	$12.00

Payment expected upon completion of job.

addressed to your customer. If you have a contract, the information you need for the invoice can be taken right from the contract.

Whether you are providing a service or selling a product, some customers may want a receipt. A receipt is a written document that shows what was purchased, how much was paid and the balance owing, if any. Receipts can be handwritten or you can preprint several copies and then fill in the details when you've been paid. A receipt should be dated but does not have to be signed.

Receipt		12/6/1996
12 Cookies @ 65¢/ea.	$7.80	
Amount Received	$7.80	
Balance owing	0	

Contracts, invoices and receipts are the written documents you should be familiar with. Of course, you do not have to use any of these documents for your business. It will be up to you to decide which are important for your customers and for your own record-keeping.

YOUR RESPONSIBILITIES

Before you start work, you have to make sure you have the skills you need to do the job right. Many parents feel more comfortable with a baby-sitter who has taken a course in baby-sitting and first aid. Kids with successful baby-sitting businesses often start as mother's helpers and have glowing references to prove they do a good job.

Whether you are in business for yourself or doing a one-time job for someone, you need to do the job with a sense of purpose and responsibility.

What are some of the responsibilities you have as an employee or as a business owner? You need to:

- understand exactly what the job involves

- complete the job as promised

- do the best possible job

- show up on time

- tell your employer/customer about any restrictions you have, such as the time you have to be home

- call promptly if you cannot show up for work on a particular day (and perhaps, find an acceptable substitute you can offer as an option)

- find out how often and when you will be paid

- talk about any problems you are having with your employer or customer

Your responsibilities don't end there. You also have responsibilities to yourself and your parents. Before you consider taking a job or starting your own business, think about some of these things:

- How many hours each week will you have to work? What days of the week?

- Will your paying job interfere with your school commitments?

- Will you still have time for your friends?

- Will your work conflict with family plans?

- How will you get to your job, and how will you get home?

SELF-EMPLOYMENT IS NOT FOR EVERYONE

Not everyone is cut out to be in business for herself. If you would rather just get a job, then just get a job. There are lots of places to find jobs you may enjoy. Ask your parents for things you can do around your home for earning some extra money. Ask neighbours and friends if they have things they need done. Look at the bulletin board in the supermarket to see if there is something that interests you. Consider sticking up a card of your own to advertise what you are willing to work at. Check the local newspaper ads. You might even consider volunteering your services. For example, if you really like younger kids, you could volunteer at a local day camp. If you love animals, volunteer at the humane society or the local pet store. Who knows, eventually it could lead to a paying job. In the meantime you will be developing your skills and building good references.

HELPING YOUR KIDS TO PROBLEM-SOLVE

When your children enter the "real world" of working, they are bound to face the occasional dilemma or awkward situation that must be resolved. Here are a few that may crop up. Even if they don't, they should make for interesting discussions.

- You walk the dog of an elderly neighbour, Mrs. Zolt. You are allowed to walk anywhere in the neighbourhood, providing you do not cross Elm and Willow, the two busiest streets. Mrs. Zolt needs milk and bread from the store and has asked you to run her errand while you walk the dog. But the only store requires that you cross Elm Street. What do you do?

- You have been mowing Mr. Wilson's lawn for several weeks. Mr. Wilson now says that he cannot afford to pay you what you originally agreed to. What do you do?

- At your lemonade stand, a customer gives you too much money and begins to walk away before receiving his change. What do you do?

- You agreed to clean out Mrs. Wilson's garage. Now you've found out Mrs. Wilson also expects you to wash her car. What do you do?

- You go into a store and buy an item. The cashier gives you too much change. When you begin to tell her she has made a mistake, she shoos you away. What do you do?

- You've been sitting at your cookie stand all day. You've sold only two cookies for a grand total of $1. A passerby stops, samples a cookie and says it's delicious. She buys every last cookie you have — all 38 remaining. Giving you $20, she tells you to keep the change. As she begins to walk away, she suddenly turns back and asks if there is any peanut butter in the cookie. She says both her children are allergic to peanut butter. You did use peanut butter, but not much. What do you say?

- You're almost finished setting up your lemonade stand. Suddenly you realize you don't have any more sugar. You know that your parents keep $10 in the kitchen drawer for emergencies. They're not home. What do you do?

- You're supposed to baby-sit tonight. Your girlfriend calls and tells you about a party you just have to go to. What do you do?

- Mrs. Zolt is supposed to pay you every week when you finish walking her dog. She hasn't paid you for three weeks because each time she hasn't had sufficient money on hand or hasn't had change. What do you do?

PARENTS, A FINAL NOTE ON ENTREPRENEURSHIP

While your kids may be able to come up with dozens of ways to earn money, you'll usually have to help them turn their ideas into a learning experience. The words you use to communicate with your kids will have an important effect on their decisions to forge ahead or give up. While they won't always make money from their ventures, with your help they'll be able to identify what it takes to be productive.

Children should be encouraged to measure their success in more terms than simply the amount of money they made. The skills they learn and their experiences are just as important. Help your children to see the positives in all their ventures.

Even if you think their idea is destined to fail, your children still have the right to try and to learn from their mistakes. I-told-you-so's are never positive, so avoid them at all costs. Entrepreneurship is often a matter of trial and error. But an entrepreneurial spirit is natural since most children want to create. Unfortunately even the smallest failures can quickly wipe out the bravado it takes to make the leap from dreamer to doer. You play an important role in encouraging your children's natural desire to be entrepreneurs.

Wilson Harrell, a speaker and consultant to the entrepreneurial market, tells the story of how his father helped him to become an entrepreneur. "When I was six, I founded my first enterprise, a lemonade stand. My father gave me the capital to buy lemons and sugar. I furnished the labour. Every month we split the profits at a formal, sitdown business meeting. When I gave my father his share, I felt nine feet tall. I ended up with six lemonade stands and a bank account in my name. At age seven, I bought him out."

Tell your children how proud you are — and how proud they should be — of their efforts. Give them responsibility and encouragement. Make them accountable. If you put money into a new venture, it's your job to ensure your child recognizes the importance of sharing profits and repaying the loan. Reinforce your kids' need to try new things and help them to see the positives in their experiences. You will be helping them to become brave and willing triers-of-new-things. That's what entrepreneurship is all about.

MONEY DOES NOT EQUAL HAPPINESS

Young people hear adults say a lot of things that can be confusing or deliver mixed messages about just how important money is. Some people may say things that lead youngsters to believe that when you have enough money, life will be wonderful. Or that when you have your own money, you'll be in control of your destiny. Phrases such as "money talks," "money makes the world go round" and "filthy rich" convey ideas about money and value.

Having a lot of money may mean you never have to work again. But sitting around all day doing nothing won't make you happy. To be happy, you need to be motivated, challenged and always learning new things. While the idea of just being able to go out and buy anything you want may seem really interesting as you imagine it, it's less fulfilling once you've done it. And having a lot of money doesn't guarantee that you'll even spend it. Remember miserable old Mr. Scrooge in Charles Dickens's *A Christmas Carol*? Despite being filthy rich, he wasn't very happy.

While people who have a lot of money may seem to get more respect in our society, having lots of money doesn't ensure you have a loving family or good friends. Often wealthy children feel lonely. Phrases such as "poor little rich girl" have been used to describe very rich people because, despite their wealth, they don't have a very happy family life. Love and friendship come from responding in caring ways to the people in your life, not from buying them expensive gifts or always offering to be the one who buys lunch for the gang. The unfortunate truth is that people who "buy" their friends often find themselves without friends when their money runs out or when someone with more money comes along.

Some people use the money they have to draw attention to those who have less. Some use their money for power or control. Some adopt a superior or condescending attitude. All of these are usually indications that those people are insecure within themselves. Money itself has no inherent value. Money is simply a means of exchange. Having more money doesn't make one person better than another; it simply means that person can buy more stuff.

DISCUSSION POINTS:

Think of a job you had to do, for which you were paid, but really hated. Was it worth the money to have to do the job? Why or why not?

If you were paid more money, would that have made the job easier?

If you were asked to do the job for no money at all, would you do it?

If you were asked to do the job again and were offered twice as much money, would you take the job?

*What **wouldn't** you do, regardless of how much money you were offered?*

If you had more money than you could ever spend...
What would change in your life?
What would you do with the rest of your life?
What would you do with your money?
How would you make sure you were happy?

MONEY LESSON
(AGE 11+)

The objective of this exercise is to create an open discussion so you and your children can begin to clearly see what your attitudes towards money are. You may also want to include people like grandparents, aunts and friends in this activity to make the discussion lively and to cover as many different perspectives as possible.

Read the following quotes about money and ask your children to tell you:

a) what they think the person meant
b) how they feel about the quote

1. When money talks, there are few interruptions. (Herbert Prochnow)

2. What this country needs is a good five-cent nickel. (Franklin P. Adams)

3. He that makes money before he gets wit will be but a short while the master of it. (Thomas Fuller)

4. A penny will hide the biggest star in the universe if you hold it close enough to your eye. (Samuel Grafton)

5. The plainest print cannot be read through a gold eagle. (Abraham Lincoln)

6. But the jiggling of the guinea heals the hurt that Honor feels. (Alfred Lord Tennyson)

7. Money is what you'd get on beautifully without if only other people weren't so crazy about it. (Margaret Case Harriman)

8. I don't like it [money] actually, but it quiets my nerves. (Joe Louis)

9. When a man says money can do everything, that settles it; he hasn't any. (Edgar W. Howe)

10. It's good to have money and the things that money can buy, but it's good, too, to check up once in a while and make sure that you haven't lost the things money can't buy. (George Horace Lorimer)

6 DEVELOPING A SPENDING PLAN

Once they've learned what money is and how to get it, children also need to learn how to keep it. We've all used the expression "Easy come, easy go." Many people who make lots of money in the end have absolutely no idea where it's gone. People who don't have a spending plan and who don't track their income and expenses sometimes wake up to find they have little or nothing to show for their years of hard work.

As soon as I got my first real job and was responsible for my own keep, I made a budget. I had to. I didn't make enough as a legal secretary to allow me to let a single penny slip through the cracks. I lived from one pay to the next, grateful that I was able to make it through the week without disaster. I had no savings, and no idea what I would do if some unexpected expense arose. I had just enough to make my rent, eat pretty basic meals, and get to and from work. If I needed new shoes, I had to plan way ahead to be able to afford them. I didn't have a charge card (thank heavens) and, bless her heart, my mother had instilled in me a distinct hatred of borrowing.

I vividly remember sitting down and planning what I would do if I ever made $30,000 a year. I would be rich. I could afford so much more. I wouldn't have to scrimp, I could buy just about anything I wanted, and I'd be able to set aside money to keep me safe.

Not surprisingly, by the time I achieved my goal of making $30,000, my expenses had risen dramatically. Since I was in sales, I needed a car. I had to add car payments, insurance payments, gas and repairs to my spending plan. And I had to expand my wardrobe. Expenses are a little like water. As long as they have someplace to go — which is usually up — they keep moving. While I had committed to putting aside some money each month for savings, I wasn't rich. I wasn't scrimping anymore, but I still had to watch my financial diet very carefully. A single overindulgence could take months to repair.

Thankfully, my income continued to increase as I moved from career to career. But those early lessons in money management served me well in terms of keeping my perspective clear. Once or twice I jumped off track in a big way, but I was always able to restabilize myself, get back on track and keep going. I expect the remainder of my life will be very similar. I still use a spending plan, keep track of expenses and plan ahead for major bills. I've accepted the fact that no matter how much I make, I will still live up to my means.

WHAT IS A SPENDING PLAN?

A spending plan, or budget, is a way of keeping track of the money you get and the money you spend. The best thing about a spending plan is that it gives you a very clear picture of your financial reality. When you do all your money management in your head, it's very easy to forget things — sometimes important things — that will have an impact on your overall financial plan. If, for example, you write cheques without recording what you've paid for, it's easy to forget how much you've spent. You're always guessing how much you have left.

People sometimes cringe when I talk about the need for a budget, which is one reason I use the term "spending plan." They relate a budget with having to give up things that let them enjoy life. They think that if they go on a budget, they will never again have any fun. In reality, a spending plan gives you the *freedom* to enjoy yourself, because you don't have to worry about how you'll pay the bill when it comes in. You'll know, right from the start, whether you can afford the purchase or not.

A lot of people believe budgets don't work and, as with any self-fulfilling prophesy, for them this is true. While a major emergency such as sudden unemployment can put a real crimp in any budget, even that can be overcome with a spending plan that puts aside money each month for an emergency. The reason budgets usually don't work is because people either don't have the commitment to stick with them, or because they set unrealistic goals, which doom them to failure.

People who barely make it from one paycheque to the next are often surprised when they take the time to do a spending plan. Tracking how their money flows in and out helps them clearly see where that money is going. They may not have realized just how much they spend on impulse purchases, lunches or drinks with friends. Just as importantly, they usually find it much easier to reach their goals when they have a plan to work with.

Think of a spending plan as an architectural drawing. Without one, you may build too big a bathroom and end up not having enough space for all the bedrooms you need. Or you might put the staircase in the wrong place. Maybe you won't remember to put in enough windows. Your rooms will be dark and you'll have to spend more money on lighting. Or perhaps you'll completely forget to build in closets. With a spending plan, as with an architectural drawing, the first thing you do is think about all the must-haves. Then you have the flexibility to build in the want-to-haves. You'll know your rent is covered each month, so you won't be evicted and have to spend extra money moving from one place to another. You'll know just how much you can afford to spend on food, so you won't eat steak for the first three days of the month and then live on macaroni and tuna for the remainder of the month. You'll know just how much you can afford to spend on transportation, so you can decide whether you can afford to indulge yourself in a cab ride without having to walk to work for the next four days.

KIDS AND SPENDING PLANS

Once you start your child on an allowance, your next job is to help him establish a spending plan so he can see how that money should be managed. If you don't help your child to establish a spending plan, you will not have much recourse when he spends all his allowance in the video arcade and then hits you up for bus fare to get to school. If you don't take the time to teach the important skill of planning, you leave your child to learn about a spending plan the hard way: trial and error. We all have to learn to discipline our urges for instant gratification. A spending plan helps children see the consequences of spending money.

Your child will still make mistakes. It takes time to get the concept of a spending plan down. But at least he'll have a framework within which to work. Using such a framework, rather than relying on hit and miss, will result in far more effective learning — and be a lot easier on you.

The first question you may face when you suggest setting up a spending plan is "Why?" Here's the answer: "A spending plan lets you pay for the things you need and save up for the things you want." While there are other components to a spending plan, these are the two that hold the greatest meaning for kids.

At this point you need to explain the concepts of saving, spending (mad money and planned spending) and sharing. You may have just started giving your child an allowance (or you may have done this some time ago), part of which may include money for things you expect her to pay for herself. Now you need to establish what the spending plan will look like.

If your child has already been receiving money and has no spending plan, (particularly if you've been using the dole system), you may have to take her through the exercise of writing down how much she receives and what she spends her money on now. Often children who already have an income may not be aware of how much they get and how they spend it. If this is true of your child, your first step will be to help her itemize the income she receives (she may be very surprised at just how much she gets) and how she's spending it.

MONEY LESSON
(AGE 10+)

Using a photocopy of the sample spending plan on the following page, explain each section of the plan.

1) Income: This is the money your child receives as an allowance and/or he earns.

   Should money received as a gift be included in this plan? Yes, but only to the extent that it may help your child meet one of his planned spending goals. Money received as a gift shouldn't come under the same rules and regs as other money, since it is not really income. If your child had received an actual present, that would not have applied to the spending plan, so birthday and other holiday money should not be included unless your child wishes to do so.

Spending Plan

	A Planned	B Actual	C Difference
1. Income:			
_____	$	$	$
_____	$	$	$
_____	$	$	$
2. Expenses:			
_____	$	$	$
_____	$	$	$
_____	$	$	$
_____	$	$	$
_____	$	$	$
3. Savings:			
_____	$	$	$
4. Planned Spending:			
Expenses (from above)	$	$	$
_____	$	$	$
_____	$	$	$
_____	$	$	$
5. Sharing:			
_____	$	$	$
6. Mad money:			
_____	$	$	$

2) Expenses: These are the items for which your child will
   have to pay. If you've included bus fare and lunch money
   as part his allowance, these should be listed under
   expenses.

   You may have to help your child brainstorm the expenses
   he has. Using the mind-mapping procedure described in
   chapter 5, begin by helping him to identify the things he
   likes to do. Then help him to determine which items
   involve regular expenses. For example, if your child
   collects comic books, he may wish to budget a specific
   amount each month for his comic-book collection. If he is
   an avid skier, he will have to put aside money for
   equipment and lift fees.

3) Savings: Having decided to get your kid into the savings
   habit (see chapter 7), you need to explain why he should
   save and the amount he should save. The general rule of
   thumb is that everyone — children and adults alike —
   should save ten percent of their income. In the case of
   adults, this is usually put towards things like emergency
   funds and retirement planning. In the case of kids, an
   emergency fund is still a good idea. The other long, long-
   term goal may be a college education.

4) Planned Spending: This includes the amount listed under
   Expenses, as well as any goals your child has.

   This is a good place to talk about your child's goals.
   Perhaps he wants to buy a puppy. Maybe he wants to buy
   a new bike, yet another Sega game or a special article of
   clothing. (See Setting Goals on page 93.)

   Planned spending should also include things such as
   putting aside money for the purchase of gifts if your child
   is expected to buy his own presents. It may also include

money that must be put aside for year-long purchases. For example, if your child is expected to buy a certain amount of his own clothes during the year, his planned spending list has to reflect this.

5) Sharing: If it is important to you that your child develop the habit of sharing, now's the time to talk about it. The rule of thumb for sharing is five to ten percent of income.

6) Mad money: Whatever is left after the spending plan is made should be considered mad money to be spent in any way your child wants. Every spending plan should contain at least a small amount of mad money. While you may argue that you don't have the privilege of having mad money yourself (and you think it sets an unrealistic expectation), remember your child is still just a child. The rest of the money lessons will be quite sufficient to teach him the things he needs to know about money management. Building some mad money into the spending plan helps keeps the whole process of learning about money fun.

Remember, too, that you are under no obligation to fund your child's mad money. If you think it's appropriate that he work for his mad money, that's fine. Just ensure that you are providing sufficient financial support in the other areas so that his mad money isn't eaten away by fixed expenses.

Now the columns:

A. *Planned* is the money your child plans to spend on each of these areas. For example, if your child receives a clothing allowance as part of his overall allowance, under this planned spending heading he will have itemized "clothing."

Under the *planned* column, he should include the amount of his clothing allowance.

B. *Actual* shows where the money actually goes. For example, the spending plan may call for your child to put aside five dollars each week in planned spending towards a new Sega game. However, she may have found herself with an unusual expense in one month. Perhaps she needed extra money for a gift. So, she may actually have put nothing away for the Sega that week, but would have put an extra five dollars in the *actual* column for gifts.

C. *Difference* is the difference between what was planned and the actual amount spent. For example, if your child intended to spend two dollars a day on lunch, but brown-bagged it for the week instead, his *planned* would be ten dollars, his *actual* would be zero and the *difference* would be ten dollars followed by a plus (+) sign to show he was under budget.

If he planned to spend five dollars on a gift for a friend's birthday, but spent seven dollars (which would go under *actual*), the difference would be two dollars followed by a minus (-) sign to indicate he exceeded his budget.

Help your child establish a spending plan of her own. She can fill in the photocopy of the sample budget, or you can use it as a guide to help her create her own spending plan. If this is your child's first experience with a budget, estimate the likely amounts for each item and agree to track them for a few weeks. Then sit down and redo the plan based on the realities of your child's life. (Be prepared. You may find you have to give your child more for fixed expenses because you may have underestimated.)

Children under 11 may not be able to handle this complex version of a spending plan. For younger children or children just getting used to having money of their own, you may wish to simply explain the need to save, share and plan for spending (although, initially, most of their spending will be impulsive). Label three containers "save," "share" and "spend," and each time you give your child her allowance, remind her (do it with her) to put the appropriate amounts in the savings and sharing containers. She can keep the rest in the spending container. Reinforce that when the money in the spending container runs out, that's it until she receives her next allowance, so she should keep that in mind when deciding whether to buy something.

One more thing. Some parents feel that if a child hasn't spent everything allocated in expenses in one time frame, that money should be reallocated to savings or the allowance should be reduced. Don't do it. Corporations and government today are suffering terribly from just such an approach to budgeting. Departments rush out at the end of each fiscal year to spend all the remaining money in their budgets, rather than saving it for worthwhile expenses in another time frame, for fear that that will lose part of their budgets the next year.

Your child's wise consumer habits should be rewarded, not punished. I suggest, instead, that you match whatever your child has managed to save on her expenses and move the whole amount into planned spending for a special treat.

CHILDREN WHO BLOW THEIR BUDGETS

Let's say your kid just doesn't get it. Every week, all the money you give for allowance is spent almost immediately. She doesn't have enough left to pay her own expenses. She doesn't put anything aside for sharing or saving. She simply spends it all.

Whatever you do, don't take away the allowance with an "Oh you're impossible. If you're going to act like a baby, I'll just have to dole it out to you like a baby." On top of the negative impact on her self-esteem, such an action removes her responsibility to learn about money management and places it squarely back on your shoulders.

Begin by asking your child why she is finding it difficult to stick with the spending plan. Listen to what she has to say. You may find that your child is simply not mature enough to handle money using a spending plan. If so, you could use the three-containers approach. Periodically remind your child that you are ready to move to the more sophisticated spending plan approach as soon as she's ready. Keep your eyes and ears open for signals that she wants more responsibility. And keep the channels of communication open. Be supportive and reinforce her saving and sharing efforts by helping her to count out how much she has put aside. Eventually she'll want to take over the management of her own spending plan.

KIDS WHO LOSE MONEY

Every parent in the world has probably heard about the child who comes home without his allowance. "Where's the money I gave you this morning?" His reply: "I lost it." Should you replace it? Maybe, but you have to walk a fine line in doing so.

The first time this happens, talk about how the money was lost and how he might avoid losing money in the future. Help him to identify a safe place to keep his money, stress the importance of not walking around with all of it in his pocket, and make sure he has a wallet to keep it in. Replace his allowance.

If it happens again, talk about how it happened, but only replace the portion of the money that will cover such expenses as bus fare. Don't replace his spending money. The only way for your child to realize the real impact is to have to do without at least a portion of the money he lost. Replace the funds he needs to meet his expenses in one lump sum and reinforce how important it is to keep it in a safe place.

If your child continues to lose his allowance, here are some options you can try to make the point that losing money has a consequence:

- Tell him he will continue to receive the same amount of allowance, but that for the next week you will give him the appropriate amount each day. Then stretch it to every two days, every three days and so on till you are back on the once-a-week schedule.

- Insist that your child do some paid work to replace the lost allowance.

- Let him borrow the amount he needs to at least meet his expenses. Have him sign an IOU and charge him interest on the amount. Unfortunately it will have to be interest at an exorbitant rate or the lesson won't be brought home. Let's face it, at ten percent, the interest on a dollar is only ten cents for an entire year, which will hardly make the point. Consider using a fixed-fee amount (such as a dollar) each time you have to lend your child money to replace money that has been lost.

DEALING WITH UNUSUAL EXPENSES

From time to time your children will come to you with requests for extra money to cover unexpected or unusual expenses. For example, if a friend is leaving town and there's a big going-away party, your child will want to participate. Or perhaps there's a special ski trip being planned at school. Whatever the case, you'll have to make a decision about whether to help fund these special occasions.

If your child has been prudent with her spending plan, you may decide to use such an occasion to reinforce her efforts by offering to give her the money for this special event. Another alternative would be to offer her the opportunity to earn extra money (or point out jobs she can do outside your home). You might also want to consider sharing the cost of such special events with your child. Tell her you'll kick in half the money she needs if she can come up with the rest.

SETTING GOALS

Part of helping your child to see the value in a spending plan, particularly the category "planned spending," involves being able to identify her goals.

Children wish for things all the time. "I wish I had a new bike," "I wish you'd let me buy my own clothes," "I wish I could buy Dad a really great birthday present." It's easy to wish, but if you really want to make a wish come true (as opposed to simply dreaming), then you have to develop a plan to make that wish a reality. When you do, you've set a goal.

MONEY LESSON
(AGE 6+)

Charting is an excellent way to help young children stay on track towards a goal. Ask your child to choose an item that she will have to set aside money each week to buy. Create a chart to help her visualize how setting aside money each week will help her to achieve her goal.

1. How much does the item cost? For example, let's say the item costs five dollars (including sales tax).

2. How long — and how much — will your child have to save to buy the item? If she decides she can save a dollar a week, it will take five weeks to save enough to buy the item.

3. Find a picture that represents the item your child wishes to buy and paste it at the top of the chart.

4. Draw five squares on the chart and in each square write the amount your child has to save.

5. Staple or glue an envelope to the chart. Each week, when your child puts the amount she is setting aside into the envelope, she can mark off one of the squares. This will help her to see that she is getting closer to her goal.

6. When she puts the last dollar in the envelope, celebrate her success in accomplishing her goal. Take her shopping so she can buy the item she's been saving for.

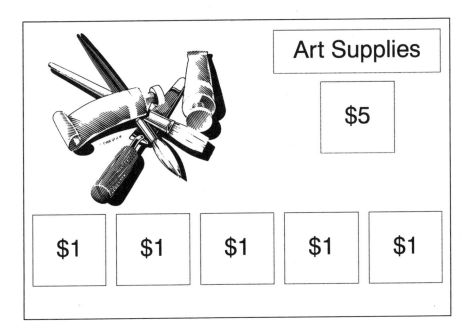

MONEY LESSON
(AGE 8+)

Ask your child to list all the things she would like to have. Write her responses on a large sheet of paper. Then ask her what things she would like to do. List those answers, too.

Now, go back over the lists and ask her which items she's prepared to work for to achieve. Point out that satisfying a goal doesn't happen overnight; that it takes time, a plan and effort.

Choose one goal from your child's list. Ask her for ideas on how she's going to make her wish come true. These ideas will be the steps in your child's plan.

For example, if your child wants to learn to play the piano, some of the things she will have to do are:
- get the money for piano lessons
- find a piano teacher
- arrange to take lessons
- decide how she will get to and from her lessons
- arrange her schedule to accommodate her lessons

If you child wants to buy the latest and most trendy pair of jeans, she might have to:
- find out who sell those types of jeans
- find out the normal price of those jeans
- decide how much she wants to set aside each week for the jeans
- comparison shop for the best price
- go and buy the jeans

Once your child achieves a goal, give her lots of positive reinforcement. Tell her how proud she should be of herself for setting and achieving her goal. Ask her what she plans to do next. Encourage her to keep striving. And also encourage her to balance her "acquisition" goals with other types of goals.

When children have set goals to work towards, it's much easier for them to give up the things that are less important. It's also easier to identify spending that "wastes" money because it does nothing to help achieve the goal. Children are usually happy when working toward a goal, and the sense of achievement they get fills them with pride and drives them on to the next goal.

7 KEEPING MONEY

So now that the kid has some money and has started to put some aside in "savings," you will likely have to do a little reinforcing of the savings habit to make it stick. Parents have complained for an eternity that they can't get their kids to save. As soon as a decent sum is accumulated, it disappears into the purchase of the latest trendy item. Or children simply refuse to save because "it's my money and I can do whatever I want with it." These children are simply a reflection of our society today.

One well-intentioned piece of advice offered by determined parents and concerned money specialists alike is that you simply must make your child save. The theory is that once they develop the savings habit, it will last a lifetime. Bullying may work in terms of keeping the money in the bank, but it does nothing to help children develop their own motivations for saving. Some habits simply don't outlast our parental influence. So while the idea of putting money in the savings container regularly is a good one, the lesson in saving can't stop there.

WHY DO PEOPLE SAVE?

Adults save for all sorts of reasons. They save to have a nest-egg for retirement. They save to ensure they have a safety net should disaster strike in the form of unemployment or unforeseen expenses. They save to be able to buy things at some later date. However, most children will place little importance on the need to save without some explicit direction. Kids simply don't have the same concept of time we do. It's virtually impossible to explain the importance of saving for retirement to a child. After all, to a seven- or eight-year-old, a year seems like a lifetime.

With the right attitude and approach, saving can be as easy and as rewarding as spending. As a child, I enjoyed the feeling of watching my savings grow. After my dad opened up my first bank account, I was thrilled with the whole concept of interest and the fact that my money made more money without my having to do a single lick of work. It seemed like magic. And it felt good. I began saving for retirement in a tax-deferred plan when I was 22. The idea that the tax man would give me back money for saving for my retirement seemed too good to pass up. It felt a lot like the "matching" agreement my dad and I had made.

Our children's attitudes and commitment to saving will have a significant impact on their future lives. As we watch the economy change, rising and falling on what seem to many of us like whims, we often feel out of control and at risk. And we know that many of the social safety nets that have been in place for years are either being drastically reduced or totally eliminated. The fact of the matter is, if we do not manage our money for all eventualities — including the worst of our worse-case scenarios — we may find ourselves in a very tenuous financial position. And if we don't teach our children how to prepare for emergencies, save for the future and develop an attitude of complete self-reliance, we may be dooming them to a similar fate.

DISCUSSION POINTS:
What kinds of things do adults save for?
What kinds of things should you be saving for?

A SAVINGS-MATCHING PROGRAM

One way to reward and motivate a child to get into the savings habit is with a savings-matching program. You offer to match every dollar your child saves within a specific period of time with a dollar of your own. Alternatively, you might offer to match her savings if she can save a specific amount by a certain date. "Molly, now that you're working regularly (or getting a higher allowance), you may want to consider saving a little more of your money. Here's the deal. If you can save sixty dollars by the end of the summer, I'll match that amount so you can begin investing."

A matching program also works well for planned spending on a big-ticket item. Most of us want our kids to have their heart's desires, but we also have to live on a budget. Sometimes we simply can't afford new skis, riding lessons or a computer. If your child is determined to achieve a specific goal, rather than pulling in your belt to make it happen, offer to help her by matching her savings dollar for dollar. This will help her stay focused, particularly if her goal may take some time to achieve.

Before you begin, both of you should agree on what you're saving for. Set a time limit and decide where the money will be kept. You might even want to go the extra step and sign a contract stating the terms of the program. And help your child see how well she's doing in achieving her goal by prominently displaying a record of her progress.

Of course, a matching program can take many forms. You might decide that if your daughter needs a new outfit for a special occasion, as long as she budgets carefully and puts aside the money she needs for the outfit, you'll spring for the shoes. Or if your son decides he wants to learn to play the keyboard, you'll spring for half the cost of the instrument, providing he's saved enough for the other half and his lessons.

A matching program is an excellent way to inspire children to stay focused on a long-term goal. How you choose to implement the program will be a matter of personal preference. What's important is that your child sets a goal and actively works towards achieving that goal, and that you support his efforts.

HOW TO HANDLE A COMPULSIVE SAVER

Not a problem, right? We should all be lucky enough to have children who see the value in saving. But what if your daughter isn't buying lunch at school because she wants to save more money? Or what if she's passing up on activities such as movies and parties because she doesn't want to spend her money? For many money-hoarders, the issue isn't simply a love a saving, it's often a fear of spending. These are the children who turn into misers, who resent giving, or who become expert at manipulating others to buy them treats while their own money is safely stored somewhere.

The accumulation of money should not be an obsession for anyone, especially a child. Kids need to see that money is simply a tool. If they never use the tool, there is no point in having it. Small joys like feeding pigeons a bag a popcorn more than compensate for the money spent on the popcorn. Kids need to see that.

Take stock of how your family communicates about money. Your child's behaviour may be a reaction to constant worry about money. My husband tells the story of when my stepson Kris was five and overheard a conversation about mortgages. He became concerned about what would happen if his parents couldn't afford to pay the mortgage. Where would he live? Would they have to move? Would he still be able to go to school? He wanted to get rid of that mortgage, so he offered his savings to his parents.

You just never know what's running through those little minds. You constantly have to be on the lookout for the signals they send, and you have to deal with their issues right away. It's easy to brush them aside and say, "What a silly thing for a kid to think." That doesn't stop your kid from thinking it.

Keep your eyes open for the signs of a compulsive saver and try to modify her behaviour gently. Ask her to participate financially in a special family treat, such as going to a movie — let her buy the popcorn with her money; or going to the amusement park — let her buy some of the ride tickets for the family. Later, talk about how much fun she — and the whole family — had. Thank her for helping make it happen and reinforce that money is just a tool that can be used to have fun.

HOW TO DEAL WITH A RELUCTANT SAVER

Despite all your effort, your child still refuses to save. What can you do? Well, the first step is to try to help your child determine why he is having difficulty saving. He may have expenses that keep cropping up that don't allow him to save as planned. For example, a slew of birthdays or holidays may have depleted your child's planned spending and resulted in his dipping into savings. There are two things you can do to help remedy this type of situation:

1. Help your child re-evaluate his spending plan. Perhaps he is simply not receiving enough to meet his commitments. A friend of mine couldn't understand why her son kept dipping into his savings when he seemed to have a good handle on the concept of saving. After a review mother and son realized that the money set aside for lunch money was no longer

enough to meet his needs. Each day he was spending more than his allotment, eating into his planned savings. When Mother's Day, his sister's birthday and Father's Day came hot on the heels of one another, he had to empty his savings to buy presents. After they rejigged his allowance, the problem went away.

2. Help your child to determine where the money is being spent. It's not surprising that children feel many of the same consumer pressures adults feel when it comes to buying presents. Is this present good enough? Is a more expensive present better than a less expensive one? Does the amount spent reflect your love or regard for the person who will receive the gift? Your child may have some interesting answers to these questions, which may shed some light on the problem. (See chapter 6.)

During your discussion you might discover that the issue is your child's inability to anticipate and prepare for unexpected expenses. This, in itself, is an important lesson.

DISCUSSION POINTS
What types of unexpected expenses have you seen Mom and Dad have over the past few months?
What types of unexpected expenses have you had?
What are some other unexpected expenses you should anticipate?
What can you do to take care of these unexpected expenses without depleting your savings?

Keep in mind that your child's lack of commitment to saving may simply be a result of having too-easy access to the money. Adults play all sorts of games in order to save. They put their money in a place that makes it difficult for them to access it. They lock it up in investments that make it impossible for them to cash in and spend. They reward themselves with small treats each time a savings level is reached. They use payroll deduction or automatic investment plans so the money is taken right from their paycheques — they never see the money go, so they never miss it.

A strategy similar to one of these may work for your child. But first he must understand the importance of saving to be committed to using one of these strategies. This may be the perfect opportunity to introduce your child to the world of banking.

TO THE BANK

A bank (savings and loans, credit union or trust company) is a business that deals with money. It offers a safe place to stash your cash so that you don't have to worry about it being stolen or lost. It provides services that allow you to spend your money without ever actually touching it (cheques, credit cards and debit cards). It lends money to people so they can finance things they want to buy, such as homes and cars. It offers investment alternatives so that your money can be put to work to earn even more money.

DISCUSSION POINTS
What is a bank?
Why do people put their money in a bank?
Where would you keep your money if there were no banks?

Banking began thousands of years ago when precious metals were kept in temples. People were afraid to steal from the temples because this would anger the gods. In about A.D. 1100, banking, as we know it today, began in Italy. Since early Italian bankers did their business on a street bench or *banca*, the word "bank" become the term for the place where money was handled.

Piggy banks get their name from the type of clay that was once used to make jars. When money was stored in these jars, they were called pygg banks. Eventually the term changed to piggy banks and people began making them in the shape of pigs.

HOW BANKS PROFIT

While this is a fairly simple explanation of how banks make their money, it serves the purpose of illustrating the two primary sources of income for banks and demonstrates the relationship between the money that is placed on deposit and the money that is lent. You can refer to the diagram on the following page when explaining these concepts to your child.

1. When you deposit money in a bank, it goes into one or more of several types of banking instruments such as an account or a deposit certificate. Banks usually pay interest on those deposits. Banks make part of their profit from the fees they charge for administering the account and for some of the services people use. For example, if you want to write a cheque, a bank may charge you for processing and returning the cancelled cheque. If you want to send money to someone via a money order, there is usually a fee for this service. Since practically everyone has some dealings with a bank, the fees make up a substantial amount of a bank's money.

2. When someone asks to borrow money, and if that person qualifies, the bank lends some of the money that has been placed on deposit, charging the borrower interest for the use of the money. The interest charged on loans is always higher than the interest paid on deposit. Banks make some of their profit from the difference between the interest they pay out and they interest they take in. For example, if the bank is paying six percent on a deposit certificate and lends money at an interest rate of nine percent, the bank's profit comes from that three-percent difference. And that difference is enormous when translated into dollars.

Whenever people see the actual numbers in dollars, they are usually outraged at the amount of profit banks make, screaming blue-bloody-murder about the fees and interest they are paying, or complaining bitterly about how little interest they earn. This can lead to resentment and an adversarial attitude when dealing with banks. Before you instil hatred of the banking system in your child, here are some things to think about.

A bank, like any other business, is created to make money for its investors. If a bank does not make a profit on a pretty consistent basis, investors sell their

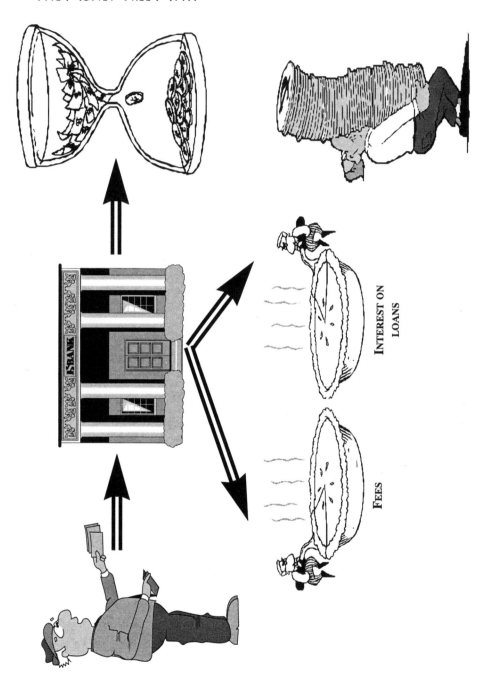

shares, and eventually the bank collapses because of a lack of funding. The result of several collapses is less competition and, therefore, less need for the remaining banks to offer competitively priced products and services.

Banks walk a pretty fine line between keeping their depositors' money safe, lending responsibly with the clear expectation of repayment, and generating profit through the interest and fees charged. And, of course, a bank is only as sound as the people who are making the decisions. Several banks have collapsed over the years because of their employees' irresponsibility in handling the bank's funds. If a lender doesn't do all the checks necessary and lends money to someone who ends up not repaying the loan, depositors are still entitled to their money. The loss has to be made up from the bank's profits. And if depositors suddenly decide that a particular bank doesn't seem safe and there is a run on withdrawals, the bank has to find a way of covering its loans (usually by borrowing money somewhere else) or it will collapse.

Of course, as with any business, it is the bank management's responsibility to ensure employees follow the rules. When banks collapse, it is often a result of mismanagement at the very highest levels.

Unfortunately the very people who mismanage one financial institution into collapse often show up managing another. This is something consumers need to watch for. If your financial institution is being run by someone who has had a bleak track record in other positions or at other financial institutions, consider moving your money. That's not to say the bank is sure to collapse, but why take the chance? All the special incentives in the world such as reduced fees or substantially higher interest rates won't make up for the loss you'll experience if your bank fails. What you want from a bank is safety, security and a well-established track record. As consumers, you also have the right to shop around and make sure you're getting the best deal going. Banking is a very competitive industry. All the concepts associated with spending wisely also apply to shopping for a financial institution. Remember, you are the customer and you have choices. Execute those choices wisely and you should have a mutually satisfying relationship with your bank.

ESTABLISHING A RELATIONSHIP WITH A BANK

When your child is about six or seven, help him establish a relationship with a bank by going on a field trip and opening up an account. Before you do, however, consider *your* relationship with your bank. Many people are intimidated by banking. They don't understand how it works, and they don't have an appreciation of how important they are as customers. You need to be comfortable to make your child comfortable. After all, you want the experience to be a positive one.

If you don't already have a well-established relationship with your banker, now's the time to start building one. Your banker should be a little like your doctor — helping you when you're financially sick and checking you over when you're healthy. You should trust your banker and feel comfortable sharing information and asking questions. And you should respect your banker enough to listen to the things he has to say.

I've had several positive relationships with banks. At one point I dealt with a branch where I was greeted wholeheartedly whenever I arrived. They asked how my baby was, whether my husband was home or travelling, and how my business was going. Every man and woman working there dealt with me as a person first and a customer second. I really liked it a lot. And I was blindly loyal, giving recommendations and referrals to this branch whenever asked. Unfortunately nothing stays the same, and over a fairly short period of time almost the entire staff of the branch changed. My relationships were gone — and so was my business.

While banks are beginning to recognize the importance of building relationships with customers, often a trip to the bank can still seem like a winding road of procedures and rules with little room for friendly exchanges. Your child may well be intimidated by the atmosphere within the bank itself. Everything will seem larger than life (you'll notice there are no counters a small child can see over), regulated and roped (I absolutely hate those cattle lines), and abrupt ("Fill out this form and sign here, give me your money and go away because I have another customer waiting.")

To create the right atmosphere for your child's first encounter with the world of banking, call ahead to your banker and explain that you want to bring your son or daughter in to open an account. Since your child is becoming a customer of the bank, he is entitled to the same attention and care that adult customers are given. If your banker doesn't want to co-operate, find another bank for your child and for yourself. Bankers claim to be committed to educating consumers. If yours isn't prepared to spend some time orienting your child to the world of banking, you can surmise that he may have little time for you if things ever get rough financially.

MONEY LESSON
(AGE 9+)

Take your child on a field trip to a bank. The objective of this trip is to introduce him to banking, help him establish his first relationship with a bank and show him some of the steps involved in banking.

Before you set off on your trip, introduce the following banking terms (if your child is not already familiar with them):

- Deposit: As a verb it refers to the act of putting money into the bank. As a noun, it refers to the sum of money being put into the bank. "When you put your money in the bank, you are depositing it. That deposit is shown right here in your passbook."

- Withdrawal: Ditto, except this refers to money coming out of the bank. "When you take money out of the bank, or withdraw it, that withdrawal is for the exact amount you want (providing you have that amount in the account)."

- Fee: Often account fees are waived on children's accounts, but your child should still be familiar with the concept. Show him a copy of your passbook or statement, highlighting the fee. Explain what the fee is for. Relate it to something your child already understands. "Banks charge fees for the services they provide. Just as you have to pay to get a haircut, you have to pay the bank to take care of your money for you."

- Interest: This is the money the bank pays you for keeping your money with them. They are going to use your money to make more money and so they pay you for the right to use your money. "Each month your bank will pay you interest on the money you have on deposit. It's sort of like renting out your money."

  Use the concept of interest to help develop and reinforce your child's motivation for saving. The idea that they get more money by putting their savings in the bank is generally quite appealing to children. Each month take your child to the bank and have his passbook updated. When you get home, look at the amount of interest earned. You may even want to create a chart that shows how much interest is earned over a year so your child can develop an appreciation of the concept of putting his money to work to earn more money. This will be particularly important when it comes time to talk about investing. (See chapter 9 for more about interest.)

- Passbook: A passbook is a printed record of all the transactions in an account. "Your passbook shows how much you have deposited, how much has been withdrawn, any interest you've earned and any fees deducted." A statement is similar except it is not in a book and the statement is usually mailed to your home on a monthly basis.

As preparation for the trip, ask your child to think of some questions about opening his account. You can help him to come up with the following list:

- How much money do I need to open an account?
- What types of accounts can I use?

- Are there any fees?
- What's the minimum amount I have to keep in the account?
- When can I withdraw my money?
- How will I know how much money I've saved?
- Will I earn any interest? How much?
- Do I have to put money in every month?
- What happens if I lose my passbook?

The idea you are trying to impart is that it takes some preparation before any important shopping expedition, and shopping for a bank account should be no different.

Once you arrive at the bank and the introductions have been made, explain what you are looking for to your banker from your child's perspective. If your child is comfortable with the idea of explaining it himself, let him do so.

Remind your child to ask the questions he developed before you arrived at the bank. You and your banker should help your child fill out the appropriate paperwork, complete a deposit slip and make the deposit. It's a good idea to start your child off with a passbook account since he then has an immediate record of his deposit. It's hard for children to put money in a bank and walk away with nothing to show for it. With him looking at the passbook, explain that the amount shown is the money he has deposited in the bank. Reinforce that the money is safe and that if he needs it, you can come back to the bank at any time and get it.

While you are at the bank, reinforce the terms you discussed with your child before going on the field trip:
- Deposit
- Withdrawal
- Fee
- Passbook
- Interest

On other trips to the bank, you can help your child discover the different services and products offered. When you make a withdrawal at an banking machine, explain what you are doing. When you go into your safety-deposit box, explain what it is and why you have one. When you buy traveller's cheques, explain the concept. When you purchase a money order, explain how it works.

Take advantage of every opportunity to widen your child's perspective on the world of money and banking. Small lessons attached to actual activities your child can watch or participate in will be much more effective than a lecture. Remember, the world is your classroom.

INTRODUCING A CHEQUING ACCOUNT

A chequing account lets you to keep your money in the bank and still use it any time you need it. With a chequing account comes additional responsibility. A cheque is a written order that directs a bank to deduct money from the specified account and pay the person or company named on the cheque.

Fun with Money ———————————— Age 9+

Children between nine and 12 may be old enough to begin learning about the concept of a chequing account. However, they are not yet quite old enough to be initiated into the world of chequing accounts at a bank. Here's how to teach the lessons at home.

Set up a banking system at home, complete with deposit and withdrawal slips, cheques and a chequebook register for recording information. You can either use materials you have gathered at your local bank, or you can make up your own (or have your kids make them up) using your own banking forms as models.

Fun with Money ———————— Cont.

Let your child deposit his allowance with you and write cheques against his deposits when he needs cash. Show him how to use the chequebook register for recording his deposits, withdrawals and cheques written. Keep a running balance for your child's account and, if necessary, bounce cheques when there are insufficient funds available. Remember to carefully explain why this happened. To encourage savings, pay interest on balances in your child's account.

If your child is already old enough to begin paying her own bills or making large purchases, explain how a chequing account works and make the trip to the bank together to set up the account. Points you should remember to cover when talking about a chequing account include:

- Always write your cheque out using ink (not a pencil) since you don't want the information to be erased or changed. What would happen if you made out a cheque for $10 and someone erased it and made it instead for $50?

- If you make a mistake, don't write over the information. (Adults do this all the time to save on rewriting the cheque, and banks will accept a changed cheque if it is initialled by the account holder. However, it is not a good idea to do this because if it happens often, it becomes hard for the bank to determine who changed the information on the cheque.) It is a much better practice to void the cheque (put a line through the cheque and write "void" across it) and write a new one.

- Always remember to fill in the date — day, month and year — you're writing the cheque.

- Write in the name of the person who is to get the money on the line that says, "Pay to the order of." You must use the person's full and proper name. What would happen if you wrote out a cheque to "Mommy"?

- Write the amount of the cheque in numbers and in words where appropriate. This is used to ensure that a cheque for 40 (forty) dollars isn't mistakenly cashed as 400 (four hundred) dollars. What might happen if you only filled in the numbers section of the cheque?

- Always sign your name after everything else has been filled out. This makes the cheque "legal tender" and gives the bank permission to cash it. Don't print your name, since your signature has to match the signature on the card you filled out and left at the bank. What could happen if you signed a cheque before you filled out the information on it?

- Never write a cheque for an amount greater than what you have in your account. This is illegal. Banks may decide to prosecute or may close the account. In any event, the shortfall will have to be repaid.

  Yes, yes, I know all about overdraft protection. But this is one of the most expensive forms of credit available, and writing NSF cheques is one of the worst habits to form. "Bouncing cheques" not only demonstrates a lack of responsibility, it also has a long-term negative impact on your credit history. Do your kid a favour. Explain the concept and then explain why it's a really bad idea.

- Each time you write a cheque, make a record of it in your cheque register or on the cheque stub. You must keep track of how much money you've spent using cheques so you can know how much money you have left in the account.

- Each month when you get your statement, compare the transactions on the statement with the record you've kept. This is called balancing, or reconciling, your chequebook.

MONEY LESSON

(AGE 14+)

Create a cheque register with entries and a bank statement that matches. The bank statement should also include a small amount of interest and a fee for the account.

Take your child through the process of balancing the statement, following these steps:

1. In the register, add in any interest shown on the statement and subtract any fees shown. Write down the new balance in the register.

2. Write down the closing the balance, which is shown on the statement.

3. Add to this any money deposited that does not yet show on the statement.

4. Subtract the amounts for cheques written that do not show on the statement. Point out that the statement is simply a snapshot of the account at a specific date and does not actually reflect the true balance, since other cheques may have gone through the account since the statement was printed.

6. Compare the final total with the number in the register. These two numbers should match. If they do not, you'll need to review the statement to see if there were cheques written or deposits made that were not recorded. When the two numbers match, this is confirmation of the amount of money in the account.

Lots of people don't use a cheque register or bother reconciling their statements. They can't be bothered with all that detail. Instead, each time they write a cheque — particularly when it's close to the end of the month — they take the chance that the cheque will bounce. One friend of mine says she has never actually bounced a cheque, but has often worried that she might. Why would ten minutes each month doing the details be worse than the anxiety and cost of an NSF cheque?

While no one may have convinced you of the benefits of taking time to record and reconcile, do your kids a favour and get them off on the right foot. Show them how, then reward them for taking care of the details.

INTRODUCING A BANKING CARD

A banking card is a small plastic card, much like a credit card, that allows access to the banking machine network. You can do almost everything at a banking machine that you can do inside a bank: make deposits and withdrawals, pay bills and transfer money from one account to another within the same bank.

Each card has a secret number assigned to it called a personal identification number, or PIN. This number is electronically encoded in the magnetic stripe on the back of the card, and the card will only work in a banking machine when this number is also used. This keeps your money safe in the event that the card is lost or stolen. It is very important that the PIN number be kept a secret. The number must be memorized and any printed record of it destroyed. Lots of people write their PIN number down somewhere in their wallet — or worse still on the card itself — only to find their bank accounts emptied when their wallets are lost or stolen.

Many banks allow the PIN number to be changed to a number that is easier to remember. This is a particularly good idea for kids who are becoming familiar with banking machines. When the number is changed, choose a number that is easy enough to remember, but not easy to guess. Your birth date or telephone number should not be used, since this information is usually also in your wallet and will be the first numbers a thief tries.

Stress to your kid that if he gives out his PIN number and his account is subsequently emptied, that's his problem to deal with. Once your child is old enough to deal with a banking card, he is also old enough to begin experiencing the consequence of these types of actions. Don't step in to remedy the problem if one does occur. There are many adults who, having not learned this lesson early enough, have lost substantial amounts of money because they didn't take the good advice given.

THE OTHER SIDE OF THE EQUATION

Of course, no review of banking is complete without looking at the flip side of the equation — borrowing. The whole area of credit is a complex one, and as such, deserves its own chapter. So you'll find everything you need to help explain credit to your children in chapter 12.

8 BORN TO SHOP!

Spending money is one of the easiest things to do. Spending wisely is not quite as easy. We've all bought things that we've looked at later and thought, now why in heaven did I buy that? The cookies smelled great, but didn't taste quite so wonderful, and the extra calories weren't worth it. That new suit looked way better in the store; in the light of reality, the colour does nothing for me. That new jukebox seemed like a great idea at the time; we just don't have anywhere to put it!

When the purchases are small, it's easy to overlook the real cost. Try adding up all those quarters spent on trivial purchases and you'll soon find dollars — even hundreds of dollars — spent, with little to show.

It's hard to deny the impact advertising has on our spending patterns. After all, if it didn't work, manufacturers simply wouldn't bother. In North America, advertisers spend billions every year creating and displaying ads designed to motivate you to spend your money. One result of advertising — impulse shopping — is a characteristic of our consumer-oriented society.

Advertising has a significant impact on children, too. All you have to do is watch your child's holiday-gift list build as the advertising pressure increases during December. Any parent who has ever been "Barneyed" knows the feeling. Regardless of where we were, at 16 months Alexandra could spot any product that had her familiar purple friend on the packaging.

Retailers and manufacturers know that children have a significant influence on how your family's dollars are spent, and so whether the product is cereal, candy or toys, they target them directly. They know the desire to acquire, and the pressure they can exert, will mean big sales.

Often the pictures and feelings ads present fall short in the light of day. Kids need help in seeing that what's presented on television isn't always what they get. When your child says he wants the latest action figure, ask him if he thinks the action figure will move by itself. When you take him to the store to buy the product, take it out of the packaging (another buy-me ploy) and ask him if it lives up to his expectations. Remind him of the concept of relative value, and that money spent now means less money available for a future purchase. Is it really worth cleaning out the garage to have those new jeans? Is he prepared to live without new sneakers until he can save up enough to get that brand-name pair worn by the famous basketball player?

Ultimately the decision to buy must remain with your child. In providing him with an allowance and with opportunities to earn money, you are giving him a way to learn about money. Making mistakes in spending is part of the process of learning. Heaven knows, as adults we make plenty of mistakes of our own.

Fun with Money — Age 10+

This is an entertaining game that can help children view commercials in a new light. Talk with your child about the different types of commercials on TV and radio. Watch or listen to several ads together and have your child label the ads. Some typical labels might include:

- Wannabe Ads: Ads showing people having lots of fun doing things many of us would love to do with a level of skill or enthusiasm most people can only dream of having — things like rafting, skiing, skateboarding, surfing, sailing, having parties, dancing. These ads are designed to make you think that if you buy the product, you'll be part of a group of fun-loving, popular achievers.

- Famous People Ads: Athletes, movie stars, musicians, famous business people, even politicians appear in ads. The message is if someone famous uses the product, shouldn't you?

- Cosy Ads: These ads depict warm, comfy pictures, usually in an intimate setting. A grandpa and grandson chatting on the telephone, best friends sharing secrets over a tub of ice cream, a man and woman holding hands as they walk along a moonlit beach. These ads want you to relate their products to love and contentment.

Fun with Money ———————— Cont.

- Facts Ads: Four out of five doctors, six out of seven dentists and nine out of ten mechanics all say this is the best product available. Could all those experts be wrong?

- Whiter-than-white Ads: Advertisers come up with all sorts of nifty ways of declaring that the product is new and improved. Is there anything that is really whiter than white?

- Everyday-word Ads: Some ads are designed to become so ingrained in our lives that we consider the product to be the only product available in that category. When you order a Coke, are you asking specifically for a Coca Cola, or will any cola do? When you ask for Kleenex, is it that specific brand you want, or are you asking for tissues? When you go to the fridge, are you opening the door of a refrigerator or a Frigidaire?

- Catchy Ads: The jingle sticks in your head and the product is the first thing that comes to mind when you think of any product in that category. Telephone numbers, catchy songs and memorable one-liners are used to firmly ingrain the product in your mind.

- The Great Offer Ads: These offer you a not-to-be-believed, too-good-to-pass-up opportunity to get more for less — eight CDs for a dollar, 12 tapes for a penny, buy two get one free, buy one and the next is half-price.

- Infomercials: This is the latest trend in advertising. Half-hour or hour-long ads, these present experts, famous people and scads of information in an attempt to convince you that you cannot live another moment without the product. And they are effective. Each of those ads usually contains a 1-800 number that provides you with the convenience of making your decision immediately. Many people do just that.

Fun with Money ——————— Cont.

Once you and your child have labelled the ads, make a game of finding four or five examples of each type of ad. Ask your child if she thinks:

- the product is better because a famous person says it is

- if she buys that product, she'll be like the people in the ad

- she'll be happier, safer, warmer, cosier, if she buys that product

- she can tell the difference between this product and a similar product. If she can't, is it worth the difference in price?

- she can figure out what the product is really like from the ad

- the deal being offered is a good deal. Does she know all the facts? Are there any catches to the deal?

- that the product would be as attractive if she took away the colourful background and sound effects

- her buying decisions are being influenced without her being aware of it

TAKING THE IMPULSE OUT OF SHOPPING

One way to avoid major shopping boo-boos is to take a time-out before you actually lay your cash on the counter. By eliminating the impulse component, you give yourself time to think about whether you really need the product. This is particularly true when there's a lot of money involved. If your response to this is, "But those shoes won't be there if I don't buy them today!" then you are an advertiser's dream come true. Fear of loss is one of the strongest motivations for impulse shopping.

Smart shopping takes time and involves some research. If a friend has the latest CD and you think you have to have it, too, borrow it first and have a listen. If you like it as much as you thought you would, shop around for the best price.

The same holds true for items you see advertised. First, check out how the product actually looks, feels and smells in the store. Next, think about what else you could buy for the same amount of money (a relative-value check). Finally, compare prices to see if the same products, or a very similar product, is less expensive in another store.

My mother-in-law is a hard-nosed shopper. All the sweet-talking sales pitches in the world just don't wash with her. In fact, the sweeter the talk, the more suspicious she becomes. One Christmas, she set off to buy my husband a new set of headphones for his stereo. I was sick of listening to Perl Jam and she was very sympathetic. In one store she was greeted by a charming young man who quickly assured her the price of the headphones she was considering was the best in the mall and that he would waive all taxes. She tilted her head to the side, smiled and said, "If that's true, young man, then I guess I'll be back to buy them," and off she set to comparison shop. She ended up buying the same headphones at another store for 25 percent less, taxes and all. Her patience and smart shopping attitude paid off.

Patience is a difficult concept for children. However, the habit of instant gratification is one that is extremely difficult to break even after we move into adulthood. While not every purchase requires deep thought and analysis — if you want that three-dollar book and you have the money, go ahead and buy it — careful consideration should be given to buying anything that costs more than a few dollars.

MONEY LESSON

(AGE 8+)

A Fun with Money exercise in chapter 3 had your child make a list of all the things she would buy if she had $100/$1000. Referring back to this list, ask your child to choose the three items most important to her from this list and answer the following questions (child's age recommendation in brackets) for each:

Is this item suitable for someone my age? (10+)

What need (want, concern, problem or desire) will it satisfy? (10+)

What else do I need to know about the item before I make my final decision? (10+)

How will I learn more about it? (10+)

Is there anything I don't like about it? (8+)

How long will I want to play with/use it? (8+)

What is the best price for it? (8+)

DISCUSSION POINT:
What are some ways you could minimize your money outlay and still get the things you want?

Put them on a gift list, wait until they go on sale, buy them second-hand, go to church or yard sales, swap an item you no longer need or want for something you do need or want (providing you have permission to do so).

SHOPPING TOGETHER

You child will take most of her cues from you when it comes to learning how to shop wisely. Remembering that the world is your classroom, you should use opportunities when you are shopping together to help your child unravel the mysteries of shopping. Here are some ideas:

121

- Ask your child to compare the contents and the price of one package or can of goods with another. Talk about how the shape and size of the package relate to the amount in the package. Talk about how to compare what you're getting for what you're paying.

- Let older children (10+) organize your coupons each month. When it's time to make the grocery list, involve your child and ask him to decide which coupons to use. In the store, let your child gather the coupon items for the shopping cart. Share the savings with your child.

- If your child takes lunch to school, have her plan her lunch menu for a couple of days (or for the whole week) and make a shopping list. Give her a set amount of money for each day (e.g., $2.00 for each day) and let her buy the items on her list during the next shopping expedition.

- On short-list shops, ask your child to guess how much the total bill will be. Another version of this is to give your child a calculator and have him keep a running total of your shopping bill.

- As you shop, discuss the things your child needs to consider. For example, when buying clothes, she needs to look at the fit, whether there is any room to grow, how well constructed the item is, the washing instructions, and the style (will it stand the test of time?).

- The next time your family intends to order in dinner, give your child a budget and ask him to manage the ordering of the meal using the takeout menu as a price guide. Each person should have an opportunity to choose at least one dish. Talk about ways to save, such as sharing an order or buying the special.

- The next time you're shopping for magazines, ask your child to decide whether it is less expensive to buy at the news stand or by subscription. What would happen if she subscribed but then didn't bother to read the magazine every month? Are there times when it makes more sense to buy a single copy rather than a subscription?

- The next time you're shopping for a household item, ask your child to help you select the item. Talk about the quality of the item in relation to its price. Is there a less expensive item that would do just as good a job? If you bought a less expensive item, would it last as long as the more expensive item?

MONEY LESSON

(AGE 8+)

Shopping for back-to-school supplies and clothes offers a great opportunity to practise wise shopping techniques.

- Ask your child to start saving back-to-school sales ads from flyers and newspapers. Have her make a list of the stores she feels offer the best deals for school supplies.

- Together, make a list of the new clothing items she will need for school. Ask her to watch the sale ads for opportunities to buy the items on her list.

- Talk about the amount of money you have available for school supplies and clothes. Look over the lists you've made together and circle the ones your child needs most.

- Based on the sales flyers, price the items you've circled first. If there is money remaining, ask your child to choose — from the items on the list — what she wants to buy with the money remaining.

WHAT'S IN A NAME?

Apparently a lot. Consumers spend billions of dollars each year on name-brand items and designer labels. The question we need to ask ourselves is, does that name brand or designer label justify the price?

Just as adults get caught up in the label game, so do kids. However, it is important for children to be able to see for themselves the relative value of buying a "name."

Peer pressure plays a big part in a child's desire for labels. Ask your child why she wants that specific item. Talk about what she's trying to achieve in buying the label. Help her to decide how important her image and what other people think are to her. Be careful in this discussion. Stock responses such as "You shouldn't care what other people think" don't serve any useful purpose. The fact that she *does* care is the issue and a stock answer won't alleviate that. What's important is that your child understands *why* she cares.

While adults don't call it peer pressure, we all know the need to dress in a costume that meets the expectations of the people with whom we deal on a day-to-day basis. If you deal with customers who wear suits, you likely wear a suit. You probably dress a certain way to go to work. Many people take great care when dressing for special occasions. These are examples of ways in which we, as adults, bow to our own types of peer pressure. And our kids pick up on this. "You can't wear that to Aunty Barb's. I'd die if anyone saw my child dress like that" sends a strong message about the importance you place on what other people think.

If your child is determined to have a label, consider sharing the cost of the item with your child. Let's say, for example, that your daughter needs a new pair of jeans. You're prepared to spend $35. She wants to buy a label costing $60. Offer to give her the $35 you intended to spend and tell her that if she can come up with the difference, she can buy the jeans she wants. Provide her with opportunities to earn the money, or help her to identify the types of jobs she can do for other people. By earning the money to make up the difference, your child will develop a sense of the relative value of the label — and whether it's worth it to her.

DEALING WITH SHOPITIS

"Shopitis," or overspending, is a problem for many people. The lure of the advertisement, the fear of losing the product if you wait, and lack of a spending plan all contribute to this rampant disease. If your child seems to be displaying the early symptoms, you need to talk about it.

A friend of mine used to complain bitterly that every time she took her son into a store, he expected her to buy something for him. "We can't go anywhere without him wanting something. Sometimes it looks like he's trying so hard to find something he can buy. I don't understand it. I don't set a bad example. I never impulse shop." This is a common complaint among parents, particularly of young kids. Where are they getting the message that they buy every time they go into a store? From you.

Think about how many times you go into a store without a specific purpose in mind. In the grocery store you buy groceries. You take your child out to buy socks and you buy socks. It's Uncle Greg's birthday next week, so you go into a store and you come out with a purchase. You're purposeful and you're committed to getting the job done.

Now, think about how often you go into a store to browse? In today's very busy world, we seldom go into a store without a specific purpose. Regardless of how careful a shopper you are, your comparison shopping and your planned spending may not be apparent to your child. All he may see is that every time you go into a store you spend money. You need to explain that there are times when you go shopping for a specific item, in which case you will likely buy that item, and there are times when you simply browse.

Take your child into stores to browse, and no matter how good a deal you see, or the strength of your desire to kill two birds with one stone, don't spend a cent. Demonstrate that when you do not have a planned purchase, you do not buy anything. Each time you take your child shopping with you, before you go into the store ask if he has an item he plans to buy and the money to buy it. Help him see that if the spending is not planned, it doesn't happen.

Ask your child to talk about why he spends so easily. Talk about how commercials increase the desire to spend. Talk about peer pressure and it's impact. Ask him for suggestions to solve his shopitis and what you can do to help him.

Be firm. If your child spends all his allowance and then wants you to buy the latest CD, say, "I'm sorry you're disappointed you can't have that new CD, but you've spent all your money and it's not in my budget." Don't give in.

If you've been giving loans or allowance advances (see chapter 4), stop. While loans and advances can serve a useful purpose in teaching children about credit, unmonitored they can also teach them credit abuse.

ALLOW YOUR CHILDREN TO LEARN

If at first your children buy lots of junk, shopping wildly from catalogues and binging every time they have money in their pockets, be patient. It takes a while to get over the heady feeling of having your own money. As your child's guide, your objective should be to point out the process, not focus strictly on the outcome. You want to help your child to develop coping skills. You want to give your child lots of practice so that making sound decisions becomes the habit. Share your own bloopers with your kids. Let them see that making mistakes is natural, but that learning from mistakes is important.

Children who are given clear and gradually expanding financial responsibility learn how to manage money. The next time you watch your child trying to decide between a piece of candy and saving for that special treat, you can smile at the great job you've done.

9 HOW MONEY GROWS

Despite the seemingly hundreds of books published on the topic of how to invest, there is remarkably little written about how various investments actually work, and the importance of understanding what you are buying *before* you buy. As adults, many of us are confused by the world of investing. We often seek help in deciding where to invest our money and we allow ourselves to be guided by advisers. Individuals who have achieved a great deal of personal success are seen as experts. However, it is important to recognize that the individuals raised to the level of financial guru have often specialized in certain types of investments. It is natural, therefore, that when they speak, their words of wisdom centre on these investments.

Like life, investing needs to be balanced. Today's best buy isn't necessarily the best buy for tomorrow. Here's an example of what I mean. The recent popularity of mutual funds has meant that more and more of our investment dollars have flooded into these investment vehicles. However, most investors know little about how mutual funds operate. They don't understand the basic premise of mutual funds, or the types of investments different mutual funds hold. And they don't understand how changes in market or economic conditions will affect their mutual-fund holdings. Even the people selling mutual funds often don't understand the basic underlying concepts and how they apply to an individual's specific needs. The result is that many people rush into investments and then rush out when the investment doesn't perform to their expectations. The proviso that most of these investments should be considered long-term investments in itself is not understood. And since many people find it difficult to deal with the whole idea of "long-term," that's not really surprising.

Once we recognize that some — not all — financial advisers have a "pet" investment, then we can view what they have to say about investing in the appropriate light. I recently attended a seminar where a very popular financial writer and speaker was promoting the importance of using mutual funds as the primary investment vehicle for retirement savings. When she was asked if bonds and certificates of deposits had a place in a retirement savings portfolio, she adamantly said no. Why? Because equity investments have historically outperformed fixed-income investments like bonds and certificates of deposit. No questions were asked about how old this investor was, how long her investment horizon was, or the types of investments and levels of risk with which she was comfortable. These are all very important considerations. Equally surprising was that no one mentioned inflation and the whole issue of real return relative to inflation — another very important consideration. Needless to say, this investor may not have received the best advice for her particular circumstances.

There are hundreds of different investment options from which you can choose when starting an investment portfolio. The most important rule in choosing an investment is:

Know what you're investing in.

If you want to expand your investment horizons, learn all about the investments you're interested in before you buy them. That means you also have to understand the factors that affect your investments.

The second important rule is:

Investor, know thyself.

If you want to be able to buy the right types of investments for your specific needs, you must also understand your personal comfort level with regard to both risk and volatility.

In teaching your kids about money, pass on these rules of investing and help them to become educated. Remember, children learn most of what they know about money from watching how we deal with money. We are their role models. If we throw our hands up in despair and say, "I'll never understand this," we send our children the message that it's perfectly okay to let someone else have control over their money and, by extension, their lives.

If you find the concept of investing a little scary, you're not alone. Many people are unsure about investing. But the concepts themselves aren't difficult to understand. It's simply that most people have not had an opportunity to

128

practise them. And unfortunately, until recently, most of what was written about these concepts used so much financial and economic jargon it seemed impossible to get a handle on them.

In this chapter and the ones following, most of the basic concepts will be covered so that you have a starting point for explaining these ideas to your kids. If you find you want to go into any of these concepts in more depth, there are lots of books available that provide good information on how money works. Developing a good understanding of investing won't necessarily mean you'll want to give up your financial adviser. But it *will* mean you'll be able to understand what she's saying so you can decide if her advice is appropriate for your particular circumstances.

PUTTING YOUR MONEY TO WORK

There are two general ways you can put your money to work to make more money. The first involves lending your money to a bank, the government or a corporation. In return, you'll be paid interest on your money. The second involves becoming an owner (or part owner) of a company by buying shares in that company.

ON BECOMING A LENDER

Most people who buy a certificate of deposit don't really think of themselves as lending their money to a bank. But that's exactly what they're doing.

When you place your money on deposit, your money isn't really sitting in the account. Your money, pooled with millions of dollars from thousands of other people, is used by the bank to provide financing to people who want to borrow to buy cars or homes or take vacations. It's much the same as if you had gone to the bank, borrowed money (on which you would pay interest) and then lent it to someone else (for which you would charge even more interest). It may not seem like lending because, of course, most people don't talk about it that way. But that's exactly what it is. You provide the bank with the money (on which they pay you interest) they can then give to someone else (for which they charge even more interest).

Whether you buy a corporate bond or a government bond, you're lending your money. The company or government body can then use that money to finance their growth or cover their expenditures. In return for the right to use your money, they guarantee you a specific rate of interest.

If you buy a mortgage-backed security, or a mortgage, bond or money-market mutual fund, the result is the same. You're lending your money, and in return you'll earn a specific amount of interest for a specific period of time.

One of the most important considerations when you decide to lend your money is how safe that money will be and how likely you are to get it back when you want it. When you lend your money to a bank, it's usually very safe because most banks insure your deposits with a government agency to reduce or eliminate your loss should something unforeseen happen. Of course, you have to be sure that your bank has deposit insurance coverage. There are now quite a few financial institutions in the U.S. that are opting out of the program. Instead they offer their depositors a higher rate of interest to make up for the fact that their money isn't guaranteed.

When you lend your money through a bond or mortgage, you can check to see how good (read "safe") an investment you're making by finding out what the credit rating is on those investments. More on this later.

ON BECOMING AN OWNER

When you become an owner, the money you spend to buy a share of a company gives you ownership in that company. If, for example, there are 1,000,000 shares outstanding for a company, and you buy one share, you own 1/1,000,000 of that company. When you are an owner, there is no guarantee you will earn a specific return on your investment. Rather, you are taking a shot that the company you have bought will do very well, and that your share will become more valuable. There's no specific time frame involved, and no guarantees. On the other hand, because you're not tied into a preset rate of interest, your investment could earn a higher return than the going rate of interest allows.

By looking at the historical performance of various types of investments, you can see just how much your money can grow. For example, if you invested $100 in 1978 in a variety of long-term world bonds, by 1993 those bonds would be worth about $600 (that's a 12-percent annual rate of return.) On the other hand, if you invested the same amount in world stocks, your $100 would have grown to $1,061 (a 16.5 percent annual rate of return.)

While ownership often has more rewards than simply lending your money, whenever you think about investing in stocks, you also have to remember that the real trick is picking the right stock at the right time. (More on stocks in the next chapter.)

WHERE TO BEGIN

Once your child has saved sufficient money to begin investing, one of the first investment vehicles usually considered is an interest-bearing investment. There are a wide variety of interest-bearing (or fixed-income) investments available, including savings accounts, treasury bills, certificates of deposit, bonds, mortgages (and derivatives such as mortgage-backed securities) and fixed-income mutual funds. These types of investments are a good first choice because the main concepts involved are pretty easy to understand. And they are relatively accessible — a certificate of deposit may be purchased with as little as $100.

One of the first concepts kids need to understand when investing in interest-bearing investments is the idea of interest and how it compounds.

WHAT IS INTEREST?

Interest is the money paid to you for allowing someone else, such as a bank or a corporation, to use your money for a specific period of time. It's like renting your money out. And you can collect the rent on your money at a variety of times. Many savings accounts pay interest daily (at least that's the way it's calculated), while other types of investments pay you monthly, quarterly or even annually.

Interest is always expressed as a percentage. So, if you're earning five percent in interest, for every dollar you lend to the bank (when you deposit your money in your savings account or buy a certificate of deposit) you will earn five cents each year in interest. The higher the percentage paid to you, the more your money will grow. Let's take the example of a kid who is 11 now and every year buys a deposit certificate of $1,000. By the time he turns 21 he will have ten certificates totalling $10,000. Now let's say each of those certificates pays an interest rate of five percent. At 21, he will have earned $3,200 in interest. If his deposit was earning eight percent in interest, his total interest would be about $5,600, and if he was earning 11 percent interest, his total interest earned would be about $8,500.

Since the higher the interest earned, the more money you get back from lending your money, it's wise to shop around and compare interest rates before you buy a certificate. After all, the objective is to make your money work as hard as possible for you.

THE MAGIC OF COMPOUND INTEREST

It isn't really magic. It just seems that way because the results can be so wonderful. Compounding means that the interest earned on an investment is reinvested so that it, in turn, can earn more interest. Over the long term (there's that word again), the increased return can be substantial.

Let's say, for example, that you invest $1,000 earning 10 percent in interest. In the first year you would earn $100 in interest. One option would be to withdraw the $100 and reinvest your $1,000. However, if you wanted your investment to compound, you would reinvest the full $1,100, which would earn $110 in interest the following year.

Of course, the more you invest and the longer you invest, the more magical compounding interest is. Let's say you invested $10,000 for five years at ten percent. If your investment did not compound, at the end of five years you would earn $5,000 in interest. If your investment did compound, you would earn $6,105 — or $1,105 more — in interest.

When you look at investing for things such as a college education or retirement, you can see just how much more you can accumulate by allowing your investment's return to compound. A $10,000 investment allowed to compound at ten percent over 25 years would grow to more than $100,000.

Compounding doesn't just apply to interest. It applies to whatever type of return your investment is earning, providing that return is reinvested. It is most often applied to interest because interest is usually paid regularly and, therefore, can be reinvested regularly to earn even more interest.

MONEY LESSON
(AGE 10+)

One of the best ways to demonstrate the impact of compounding growth is by using coins and an at-home savings plan. Become your child's banker, and each week when he puts money into his "savings," have him deposit those savings with you. Keep a written record of his deposits, and at the end of each month total up the savings and credit the interest earned on those savings. You may have to pay an astronomical amount of interest to make the exercise worthwhile, but in the short term, it will be worthwhile to prove the point.

For older children (12+), you might have them go through the exercise of calculating the return earned on money invested over ten, 20 and 30 years when the interest is allowed to compound and when it is not, so that they can see the difference in return earned.

THE RULE OF 72

There's a nifty rule you can use to determine how often your money will double when interest is allowed to compound. It's called the Rule of 72 and it works like this:

Take the interest rate you're earning on your deposit and divide it into 72. This is the number of years it will take for your money to double.

Let's say, for example, that you're earning seven percent in interest. Divide seven into 72 and you'll find that it will take 10.2 years for your money to double. If you're earning ten percent, it would take 7.2 years to double, and if you're earning 12 percent, it would take only six years for it to double.

CERTIFICATES OF DEPOSIT

Certificates of deposit are often the first investment of choice for new investors because they're so easy to understand and use. A certificate of deposit is most simply described as a deposit made for a fixed term on which you earn a guaranteed rate of interest. For example, if you choose a two-year certificate paying six percent, you would be investing your money for two years, and the six percent rate would be guaranteed for that time. Some people refer to these types of investments as CDs (short for certificates of deposit), time or term deposits (TDs) or guaranteed investment certificates (GICs).

The terms can range from as short as 30 days to five, seven or even ten years in duration. Some certificates are nonredeemable (which means you can't cash them in before the end of the term) while others are cashable whenever you need the money, usually with an interest penalty.

There are a number of special features you should look at when shopping for a certificate. For example, while some financial institutions restrict their maturity dates to annual or semiannual intervals, at others you have the flexibility to choose the exact date you want your investment to mature, although it usually has to be a business day. Many institutions offer interesting features as a way of marketing their certificates. Some allow their certificates to be transferred or cashed in prior to maturity. Others offer rising rates, which allow you to take advantage of increases in rates.

MONEY LESSON

(AGE 12+)

Once your child has a good handle on the concept of interest, it's time for a trip to the bank to learn more about how she's earning interest on her investments. This, of course, assumes she has already opened a savings account or bought a certificate of deposit.

Before you set off, you will need to help your child develop a list of questions for the banker. Here are some useful ones:

- How often will the bank credit my interest?
- What are the various rates offered on different types of investments?
- Do you pay more interest for larger deposits?
- Do you pay interest even for days that are holidays?
- If I take my money out before the end of the month, will I earn interest right up until the day I withdraw the money?
- If I cash in my certificate before the end of the term, will I lose any interest?

These questions will usually lead to some interesting discussions about things such as how:

- you can earn more interest when interest is calculated and credited more often (because of the compounding).
- different types of investments pay different rates of interest.
- larger investments usually earn more interest.
- money keeps working even when people don't.
- interest paid on average balances differs from interest paid on minimum balances.
- not keeping money in for the agreed full term results in less interest being paid.

135

THE RELATIONSHIP BETWEEN TERM AND RATE

Of course, the trick to buying certificates successfully is ensuring you choose the right term so you get the best rate for the longest possible time. The term of a certificate is the length of time the money is invested. As the terms of certificates vary, so do the rates of interest paid. This relationship is not fixed, but reflects current market conditions, as well as financial analysts' projections for future interest rates.

Sometimes the decision seems to be pretty straightforward. One-year rates are at six percent, two-year rates at seven percent, and five-year rates at eight percent. You know you won't need your money for about five years, so you choose that term to get the best rate.

A consistently increasing spread between the one-year term and the five-year term reflects a very stable market with a likelihood of increasing rates. In financial lingo this is referred to as a "normal yield curve." With a normal yield curve, the longer the term of the deposit, the higher the rate of interest earned.

Sometimes the economy goes through periods when long-term rates are lower than short-term rates. For example, while the one-year rate is at seven percent, the five-year rate is set at only six percent. This is referred to as an "inverted yield curve." With an inverted yield curve, the rate paid on longer terms (the five-year term) is lower than that paid on shorter terms (one to four years). Then you have to decide whether to take a shorter term at a higher rate and run the risk that rates will be lower when it's time to renew, or choose a longer term at a lower rate at which point you hope rates will have risen. While most people don't think there is any *risk* associated with fixed-income investments, there is, and we'll look at these risks shortly.

Sometimes the situation arises where there is little difference in the rate paid, whether the investment is for one year or for five. When interest rates paid remain the same despite the length of the deposit, this is referred to as a "flat yield curve."

The establishment of rates is far more sophisticated than this simple explanation. However, this explanation gives an insight into the different relationships that exist between term and rate.

Since rates are decided weekly (or even daily) and can vary from one financial institution to another, take the time to shop around before deciding where to make your purchase.

MONEY LESSON

(Age 12+)

Since yield curves are often represented graphically, here's an exercise to help your child develop a picture of what different yield curves look like. You'll have to do some research at the library to get samples of different types of interest-rate patterns.

Cut out samples of different types of rate patterns and paste them on a piece of construction paper. Ask your child to make a graph that is a pictorial representation of these curves. (See the following page for a sample of how this should look.) Have her label each type of yield curve.

Once your child understands that interest rates change and that there are specific names given to the way interest rates differ (the yield curves), it's a good idea to reinforce her understanding from time to time. Cut out a sample of the one- to five-year rates being offered on certificates of deposit and

- ask her to look at the spread between one-year and five-year certificates of deposit and decide what type of yield curve is in effect.

- ask her what this difference in spread says about where interest rates are headed.

A WORD OR TWO ABOUT RISK

In deciding on a term, you have to consider the risk associated with certificates. Yes, contrary to popular belief, there is a level of risk associated with this type of investment. One risk is that interest rates will rise and you will be locked in to a lower rate. Alternatively, if you've invested at a high rate, the risk is that interest rates will be significantly lower when it comes time

137

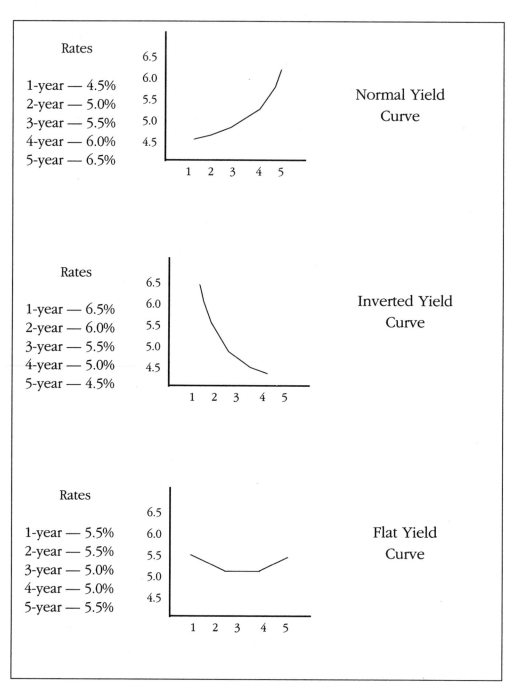

Rates

1-year — 4.5%
2-year — 5.0%
3-year — 5.5%
4-year — 6.0%
5-year — 6.5%

Normal Yield
Curve

Rates

1-year — 6.5%
2-year — 6.0%
3-year — 5.5%
4-year — 5.0%
5-year — 4.5%

Inverted Yield
Curve

Rates

1-year — 5.5%
2-year — 5.5%
3-year — 5.0%
4-year — 5.0%
5-year — 5.5%

Flat Yield
Curve

to renew. We saw this happen to people who chose to invest in five-year certificates in 1988. When it came time to renew their investments in 1993, the rates had dropped substantially.

Another risk you'll have to face is the risk that the interest rate you lock in at won't provide a sufficient hedge against inflation.

WHAT IS INFLATION?

Inflation refers to the loss of purchasing power of the dollar because of rising prices and wages, and increases in the money supply. Your child has already had an opportunity to look at the impact of inflation when she did the *Prices Just Keep Going Up* exercise on page 29.

At an inflation rate of five percent, today's $1,000 will be worth only

$613.90 in 10 years
$376.90 in 20 years
$231.40 in 30 years.

Over the past 40 years, the average annual rate of inflation has been approximately 4.5 percent. While inflation is running below that at the moment, we also have to remember back to the '80s when it raged at 14 percent. It's probably not unrealistic to expect that over the next 40 years inflation levels will be similar to those of the past 40 years.

Inflation's erosive power means that each year it becomes more and more expensive to live. Here's a way to estimate the impact of inflation on future prices.

MONEY LESSON

(AGE 14+)

One of the first long-term goals kids can set is to save enough money for their college education. The first step is to find out what it costs today to go to college. The next step is to figure out how much it will cost in the future, taking inflation into account. (As parents saving or planning to save for your child's future education, you'll find this exercise very interesting too.)

The chart on the following page will help you to estimate what today's dollar will be worth at a future date.

To use this chart, follow these steps:

1. Subtract your present age from the age you plan to go to college. Find the number in the "Years" column. For example, if you are 12 and plan to go to college at 19, you would be seven years away. So, you will use the "7" in the "Years" column.

2. Now comes the guesswork. What do you think the average rate of inflation will be over the years until you go off to college? Make your best guess by looking back over the past years and taking the average. For the sake of our example, let's assume the average rate of inflation will be four percent.

3. How much money, in today's and tomorrow's dollars, will you need? Let's assume you'll need about $10,000 a year for tuition and board in today's dollars. To translate that into tomorrow's dollars, you have to look at how much the figure needs to increase over the seven years until you actually get to college.

   Move to the right from "7" in the "Years" column to the 4% column. This tells you that seven years from now you will need $1,315.93 to buy what $1,000 buys today.

   Multiply $1,315.93 by 10 (because you need the equivalent of $10.000 a year) and you'll get $13,159.30 for that first year of college.

Inflation Equivalents of $1,000

Rate of inflation

Years	2%	4%	6%	8%	10%
1	$1,020.00	$1,040.00	$1,060.00	$1,080.00	$1,100.00
2	$1,040.40	$1,081.60	$1,123.60	$1,166.40	$1,210.00
3	$1,061.21	$1,124.86	$1,191.02	$1,259.71	$1,331.00
4	$1,082.43	$1,169.86	$1,262.48	$1,360.49	$1,464.10
5	$1,104.08	$1,216.65	$1,338.23	$1,469.33	$1,610.51
6	$1,126.16	$1,265.32	$1,418.52	$1,586.87	$1,771.56
7	$1,148.69	$1,315.93	$1,503.63	$1,713.82	$1,948.72
8	$1,171.66	$1,368.57	$1,593.85	$1,850.93	$2,143.59
9	$1,195.09	$1,423.31	$1,689.48	$1,999.00	$2,357.95
10	$1,218.99	$1,480.24	$1,790.85	$2,158.92	$2,593.74
11	$1,243.37	$1,539.45	$1,898.30	$2,331.64	$2,853.12
12	$1,268.24	$1,601.03	$2,012.20	$2,518.17	$3,138.43
13	$1,293.61	$1,665.07	$2,132.93	$2,719.62	$3,452.27
14	$1,319.48	$1,731.68	$2,260.90	$2,937.19	$3,797.50
15	$1,345.87	$1,800.94	$2,396.56	$3,172.17	$4,177.25
16	$1,372.79	$1,872.98	$2,540.35	$3,425.94	$4,594.97
17	$1,400.24	$1,947.90	$2,692.77	$3,700.02	$5,054.47
18	$1,428.25	$2,025.82	$2,854.34	$3,996.02	$5,559.92
19	$1,456.81	$2,106.85	$3,025.60	$4,315.70	$6,115.91
20	$1,485.95	$2,191.12	$3,207.14	$4,660.96	$6,727.50

Remember, this is an estimate only. To get an accurate figure, you must have a clear picture of what your expenses will be, and you'll also need to have the correct inflation rate. So, even if you're only one or two years from college, there will still be some guesswork involved.

Don't be put off by a figure that seems impossible to achieve. If anyone had told your grandmother that we'd be paying more than a dollar for a loaf of bread, she wouldn't have believed it. The important point is be prepared so that the impact of inflation doesn't come as a huge surprise.

Fun with Money ———————————— Age 11+

Want to have some fun? Try predicting what everyday purchases will cost three, four or five years from now. Once each family member has made a prediction, seal them away in envelopes and then pull them out each year to see who is closest.

Begin by making a list of ten or so common items and their cost, such as milk, eggs, a ticket to the local amusement park, a burger at your local joint, your local newspaper. Avoid things like cars, since makes and models change so frequently it's hard to compare apples with apples.

Next, each of you try to predict, without using the inflation chart, what those items will cost in a year, in three years and in five years. Then use the chart to inflate the prices based on a rate you've agreed on. If you can't agree on an inflation rate, make a note of the rate you chose on the outside of your envelope.

This is an excellent follow-up exercise that allows you to reinforce the concepts and provides you with an opening to discuss money issues at a later date.

INFLATION'S IMPACT ON YOUR MONEY'S GROWTH

The best way to describe the impact of inflation relative to earning a return on an investment is with an example. Let's say you invested $10,000 in a certificate of deposit paying 4.25 percent. During the second year of your five-year term, inflation rose to 5 percent. While your certificate will earn $425 in interest each year (assuming it isn't compounding), your net return would be less than you would need to keep pace with inflation. To be able to have the same purchasing power, you would have had to earn $500.

All these figures are net of taxes. To figure in your taxes, you would have to calculate your return after paying taxes on the interest you'd earned. With a tax rate as low as 20 percent, you would need a return of 6.25 percent on your certificate just to keep pace with inflation.

Inflation is one of the most important concepts of investing to understand. There's no point in patting yourself on the back for earning 12 percent in interest if inflation is running at 10 percent. Without considering the taxes, you've really only earned 2 percent in *real* return. On the other hand, if inflation is only running at 1.5 percent and you have a certificate paying 6.5 percent in interest, your real return is 5 percent. So, even in periods of low interest rates you can earn a good real return providing inflation isn't running rampant.

Traditionally certificates of deposit, while being easy to understand and use, have paid the lowest return relative to other types of fixed-income investments. Despite the fact that they are wildly popular — often because it takes a smaller dollar amount to buy them — people who want the stability of a interest-bearing investment should look at some of the other options available in order to earn a higher return.

While many of the following investment alternatives may not be immediately applicable to your child's investment portfolio, it's a good idea to explain how these work so that as your child becomes more proficient in handling his money, he has more alternatives from which to choose. Children 14 and older should be able to grasp the concepts behind each of the following types of investments.

TREASURY BILLS

These are short-term government-debt securities issued in large denominations. In the U.S., the minimum is usually $10,000, and in Canada they can be bought for as little as $1,000. While a treasury bill's return is based on the interest rate in effect when it's bought, there is some special investment language associated with it. Treasury bills are sold at a *discount* and mature at *par*. The difference between what you pay and what the treasury bill matures at is, in effect, the interest earned. So, if the current rate being paid is eight percent, you would pay about $925 for a treasury bill that matures at $1,000. The difference between the issue price and par will be taxed as interest on maturity. Treasury bills can be purchased for terms of between 30 days and one year. Despite the fact that they have set terms, they are completely liquid because they can be cashed in at any time without penalty. The rate of return is usually higher than the interest rates being offered on most certificates of deposits with the same term.

Keep in mind that if you pay a handling fee or commission for buying a treasury bill, this will reduce your overall return. If, for example, you buy a treasury bill for $925 that matures at $1,000 with a commission of $25, you would end up with $50 in hand, in effect reducing your return from eight percent to five percent. Because certificates of deposit have no handling fees or commissions attached to them, you can now see why they are often more popular than treasury bills. However, before you decide whether to invest in treasury bills, take the time to do the calculations to see what your return would be. And if it's higher than with a certificate of deposit, go for it!

MORTGAGE-BACKED SECURITIES

A mortgage-backed security (also referred to as a Ginnie Mae in the U.S.) is created when a lending institution pools a number of residential first mortgages and allows customers to purchase an "undivided interest" in the pool. Undivided interest means that the buyer has a claim on the cash flow, including the principal, interest, prepayments, liquidation and penalties generated by the mortgages in the pool. The claim a buyer has is proportionate to the percentage of the pool that person owns.

Let's say that a bank has pooled together several mortgages for a total pool of $500,000. If that pool is split between 50 investors, each would invest $10,000. And each investor would receive 1/50th of the cash flow from the mortgage pool.

Since mortgages traditionally earn a higher rate of interest than certificates of deposit, this is another way to earn more interest on your investment. And since mortgage-backed securities can be sold prior to maturity, they offer a high level of liquidity. However, the selling price is not guaranteed. Mortgage-backed securities, like most fixed-income investments, are interest-rate sensitive. If rates go up, the price of the mortgage-backed security will fall. This is because investors can buy higher-paying mortgage-backed securities and, therefore, have less interest in buying your lower-paying investments. As a result, if you really want to sell, you'll usually have to lower your price to make the investment attractive. The good news is if rates go down, the amount you can sell your mortgage-backed security for will rise.

The underlying mortgages in a pool of mortgage-backed securities are insured by government agencies so that both the principal and interest are fully guaranteed. This adds to the security of the investment because, should a mortgage go into default, the pool's recovery will not be dependent on the sale of the property. For this reason, mortgage-backed securities are ideal for people who want to generate a monthly income. They are available in denominations of $5,000 in Canada and $25,000 in the U.S. Tax is payable on the interest portion of the monthly payment you receive, but not on the rest.

When you use a mortgage-backed security, it's important to remember that a portion of your capital is being repaid to you with each payment you receive. So, when your $5,000 unit eventually matures, you won't receive $5,000 back. And if you've spent the portion of your principal repaid to you each month, your capital will have been reduced. If you or your child are using mortgage-backed securities to provide a steady flow of income, for example, while you are retired or when your child is attending college, you may wish to consider reinvesting the capital portion of the money you receive each month.

BONDS

A bond is a debt security issued by a corporation or government to raise funds. In effect, you are lending your money to the corporation or government and they are promising to repay your loan with a specified amount of interest. Most bonds pay a set rate of interest semiannually for the life of the bond, with the principal due at maturity.

Large corporations have found many ways of designing bonds to attract investors while keeping costs in line. These range from mortgage bonds, which corporations issue when they have adequate fixed assets to be pledged, through to debentures, which companies can issue if their financial rating is high enough to allow them to borrow without pledging any assets.

When a company does not possess fixed assets or does not wish to pledge against those assets, but is prepared instead to pledge securities, collateral trust bonds are issued. Much of the evaluation criteria for stocks would naturally apply to bonds, with one major exception: with stocks there is generally no top limit on the return generated. With bonds, however, there is a specific amount repaid at maturity and a standard amount of interest paid for the length of term the bond is held.

Bonds are rated based on the quality of the bond itself and the credit worthiness of the issuer, and usually the lower the bond's rating, the higher its yield. This is because issuers have to pay a higher rate of interest to compensate for the higher risk associated in order to attract investors. The ratings fall into two main categories and are graded on a scale: investment grade (a bond rated A or higher) and high-yield or junk bonds (a bond rated below A). While not all bonds are rated, you might want to think twice about investing in a bond that hasn't been.

Just because a bond has a good rating doesn't mean there's no risk to the investment. Bonds are susceptible not only to interest-rate risk (as all fixed-income investments are), but also to credit risk and market risk. Credit risk is the risk that the company or government who issued the bond cannot afford to repay the money borrowed. Market risk refers to the uncertainty about the future price of an investment due to changing economic conditions or unpredictable changes in investor psychology and attitudes. For example, the announcement by the federal government regarding lower-than-expected economic growth is likely to result in a broad decline in bond prices as investors lower their expectations of corporate earnings. Grave illness or assassination of a political figure can affect the general market, as well.

Since the only time interest-rate-volatility risk is a factor with a bond is when you choose to sell it before maturity, a good way to minimize this risk is to buy different terms based on your specific needs. Let's say, for example, that your daughter will be going to college in ten years. This year she could buy a bond that matures in ten years, next year she could buy a bond that matures in nine years and so on. Of course, this only works if you are reasonably sure she won't need the money earlier.

Another strategy in buying bonds takes advantage of the changes in interest rates. For example, if interest rates are currently at a high and the yield curve is inverted (indicating that all the people in the know expect rates to fall), you might decide to buy a bond now to sell it for a profit later when the rates do fall.

BOND QUOTES

When you set out to buy a bond, the price quoted is made up of a *bid* and an *asked* price. The bid is the price you would get if you were selling a bond. The asked price is what you would pay when buying a bond. Most major newspapers have daily bond quotations listed. Here's an example so you can see what all the numbers mean:

1 Issuer/Bond	2 Coupon	3 Maturity	4 Price	5 Yield	6 Change
ATT 8 1/4 24	8.25	15 Ap 24	122.80	8.094	+0.50

1. The "Issuer/Bond" category indicates who is issuing the bond. This sometimes includes the original interest rate offered (8 1/4) and the date the bond matures (2024).

2. If the original rate isn't listed under the "Issuer" category, it will be listed under "Coupon" (8.25). A bond with a coupon yield of 8.25 percent pays annual interest of $82.50. The coupon yield on a bond does not change during the life of the bond.

3. If the maturity date isn't listed under the Issuer category, it will be listed under the "Maturity" category. This bond matures April 15, 2024.

4. In this example, the price is 122.80. Usually when only one price is shown, it is the midpoint between the bid and asked prices. A full quote, in this example, might have been "122.60 bid, 123.00 asked." Despite the fact that bonds have a face value of $1,000, they are always quoted based on 100. To figure the actual value of the bond, you must multiply the quote price by 10. So in this example, the quote price would actually be $1,228.00.

5. The yield quote refers to the yield to maturity. This takes into account both the interest received when the bond comes due, as well as the difference between the current price of the bond and its price at maturity. If a bond is trading at a *premium* (or at more than par value), the yield to maturity is

less than the current yield. If the bond is trading at a *discount* (or at less than par value), the yield to maturity is more than the current yield.

The current yield on a bond is simply the annual interest divided by its current market price, multiplied by 100 to make a percentage. While the coupon yield never changes, the current yield will fluctuate based on the market price of the bond. In the case of this bond, the coupon rate is 8.25. Remember, however, that bonds always have a maturity value of $1,000. Now, let's assume the bond has been quoted at 122.80 as shown. This means its value is $1,228. The current yield is the annual interest ($82.50) divided by the current market price ($1,228), multiplied by 100 for a total of 6.71 percent. Despite the fact that the stated coupon yield is 8.25 percent, if you were to buy this bond in this market, you would earn only 6.71 percent.

6. The "Change" category simply shows the movement of the price of the bond during the most recent trading day. Again, this figure needs to be multiplied by 10 and indicates the value of the bond had increased by $5.

As you can see from this example, the yield on a bond can differ widely depending on what kind of yield we're talking about. You have to understand what return you're getting on your bond investment by understanding how the coupon yield, current yield and yield-to-maturity differ.

CALLABLE BONDS

These types of bonds can be redeemed or "called" by the issuer before they mature, usually for a stated price and at a particular time. In 1992, when interest rates fell, issuers knew they could float (or sell) new bonds with substantially lower rates, so they redeemed their callable bonds. When you're buying a bond, always check whether it is callable, and when and where. If you hold registered bonds, you will be notified of a call directly. However, if you hold bearer bonds, you need to keep on eye on the financial press so that you don't inadvertently continue expecting interest to be paid on a coupon for a bond that has been redeemed.

CONVERTIBLE BONDS

Sometimes issued by corporations, these allow you to exchange the bond for common shares of the corporation. This gives you the opportunity for capital appreciation should the common shares of the company increase in value. However, this usually means that these types of bonds pay a lower rate of interest than would a nonconvertible bond.

STRIP BONDS

When investment dealers buy blocks of long-term, high-quality government bonds, detach interest coupons from the bonds and sell the interest coupons and bond residues separately to investors at a discount, these are referred to as strip (or zero coupon) bonds. The term "strip" is an acronym for "separately traded residual and interest payments." Strip bonds provide an investment vehicle that meets investors' needs of safe, high-yield fixed-income investments that offer automatic reinvestment of interest. Often referred to as TIGRs (term investment growth receipts) or sentinals, these are secure investments that avoid the reinvesting of small amounts of semiannual earned interest. With a strip bond, you know exactly what the yield will be on your investment at the time of purchase. Maturity dates range from 60 days to 20 years.

While there is a secondary market for the liquidation of these investments, there are a few points that should be noted. If the interest rate at the time of purchase is higher than the current interest rate, it will be easy to sell the strip bond. However, if the interest rate is lower than the current interest rate, there is less likely to be a market for this investment. It will probably have to be held until maturity (or until interest rates fall below the rate guaranteed by the strip bond). Also keep in mind that strip bonds are far more susceptible to interest-rate moves than are regular bonds. This is great if you're planning to use interest-rate moves to your advantage. For example, if interest rates declined from ten percent to eight percent, the price of a conventional government bond would rise by about 20 percent. However, the equivalent strip would appreciate by about 45 percent.

Since strip bonds offer security of principal and guaranteed interest payout, they appeal to people looking for high levels of security with a better return

149

than investments such as certificates offer. However, that security should be further defined. Strip bonds issued by the federal government are very secure. Those issued by other government bodies are usually less secure and, as a compensating factor, offer a higher rate of interest.

ACCRUED INTEREST

Bonds pay out regular amounts, usually twice a year on a semiannual basis. but bond trades are constantly taking place. The registered owner of the bond at the date the interest is paid out will receive all the interest. This means if the bonds were purchased just a few days before the interest payout, most of that interest would have been earned by the previous owner, but paid to the new owner. As a result, there is a mechanism for ensuring that all bondholders receive the accrued interest to which they are entitled.

Let's suppose you have a $1,000 bond paying ten percent which you decide to sell to cousin Charlie. You sell your bond to Charlie on June 15. The next interest payment date is September 15, at which point Charlie will receive the full six-month interest payment of $50. To ensure each bondholder gets a fair share of the interest pie, however — after all, Charlie's only owned the bond for half the time — when Charlie buys the bond from you, he will also have to pay you three months' interest, or $25. You'll get your share of the interest, and so will Charlie.

FOREIGN BONDS

Just as you can play the interest-rate game to earn a higher return on your bonds, so too can you play the foreign-exchange game. Bond trading goes on 24 hours a day, every day, so there's no need to limit your bond buying to North American bonds. Foreign markets provide opportunities, as well. At any given point in time, some countries have low interest rates, while others have high rates. You can, therefore, get a higher current return on your bond investments by buying bonds denominated in other currencies. But be warned! Playing the currency game can have both a positive and a negative effect on your overall return. Make sure you seek advice from someone very knowledgeable about foreign bonds before you decide to jump in.

10 OWNING STOCKS

As mentioned in the last chapter, there are two ways to invest money to make more money: by loaning (investing in fixed-income investments) and by owning (investing in things that are expected to grow in value). Anything that has the opportunity to appreciate can be considered an investment. While most kids don't buy comic books as investments, we live in an interesting world where comic books, baseball cards and toys have taken on investment lives of their own. If you had a copy of the comic book in which Batman made his first appearance, you might be interested to learn that today that comic book is worth $66,959. And the comic book in which Superman debuted is worth $74,836!

DISCUSSION POINT
What kind of things can you buy and later sell to make a profit?

Collectables — things like comic books and art — are pretty unpredictable in terms of their investment potential. You almost need a crystal ball to decide which collectables are worth saving. Learning how to invest using shares of corporations can be much more rewarding.

WHAT ARE SHARES?

When you buy shares in a company, your ownership is represented by a stock certificate that indicates the number of shares you've bought. Common shares represent equity or ownership in a public or private corporation. So when you buy shares in Coca Cola, McDonalds or Matel, you are actually buying a piece of the company.

When a company wants to raise money to expand its business, it can do so in two ways. It can borrow money, either from a bank or from investors using things like bonds and debentures, or it can sell a part of the company to investors by issuing stock in the company. When you buy shares, you have certain rights and are entitled to share in any profit the company makes.

Stocks can make you money in two ways. If the company does well, the share's price will go up, and this increase — referred to as appreciation or a capital gain — represents the profit you would make if you sold the shares. This is the *reward* of investing. However, if the company does not do well, this is reflected in falling share prices. And if you sell when the price is lower, you will have a loss — referred to as depreciation or a capital loss. This is the *risk* of investing.

You can also make money from the dividends paid on shares. Companies often distribute the profit they make by declaring a dividend. The dividend relates directly to each share. For example, a company may declare a dividend of ten cents per share. So, the more shares you own in that company, the more dividends you will receive.

Shares are found in two different classes: common and preferred. While common-share holders have a say in how a company operates, preferred-share holders generally don't have a vote in company affairs. However, preferred shares do come first when it comes to dividend payout time. This makes preferred shares quite attractive to many investors.

Recently I met a woman who had a very interesting perspective on investing for her children. We met at a financial planning conference and she was asking for advice on her own financial position. As she described her circumstances, it became clear that she knew exactly what she was doing. She and her husband were actively saving for retirement. They were carefully balancing that with the reduction of their mortgage. Taking a stab at her age, I guessed she was about 34. Her plan had her family mortgage-free in another four years. One of the most interesting things we talked about was how she was investing for her children. She was buying shares in companies her kids could identify with — companies like McDonalds. And when she took her children to eat at Ronald's place, she impressed upon them that they owned a part of the restaurant. Chuckling, she said, "I tell them they own that chair they are sitting on because they own shares in the company."

This is one of the best ways to get kids interested in investing. By relating investing to products or services they use, you can introduce even young children to the concept of ownership and how investments grow.

And you don't have to stop there. You should also take the time to show your children how the shares they own fluctuated in value from one month to the next.

MONEY LESSON

(AGE 11+)

You can use this lesson whether you have actually invested in shares of a company or not. However, if you buy even a few shares of the companies you are working with, the lesson will be that much more interesting for your children.

Choose shares from three or four companies that are easily recognizable to your kids. Make a chart for each company. Once a month, cut out the appropriate stock listing from the newspaper and chart how the shares have risen or fallen in price. Relate the increases in price to the growth of the original sum — the capital — invested. Describe how decreases in share values mean that if the shares were sold, less money would be received. Reinforce that even if the share value falls, no money is actually lost until the shares are sold, so that by being patient and waiting for the price of the share to go up again, you can actually avoid losing money.

The concept that nothing is gained or lost until the shares in a company are actually sold seems to be one with which many people have a great deal of difficulty. When investment advisers talk about *paper* losses or gains, they are saying that these losses or gains have simply been made on paper — but that until the shares are sold, you are no further behind or ahead financially.

Some people find it difficult to get a handle on this concept. On several occasions, people have told me that they have bought investments that have fallen in value. Their question — should they sell and buy something else? I have to explain that until they sell, they haven't, in fact, lost a cent, and that by selling they are creating the loss. If the investment was made for the right reasons to begin with — if the investor did his homework and made his investment choice based on sound knowledge and facts — most often he would be much better off holding those investments until the factors that created the downturn in price corrected themselves.

A share's price is influenced by several factors, some predictable and others that cannot be foreseen. These include:

- the general economic outlook

- investors' expectations about how profitable the company will be, which translates into demand for the shares

- the company's actual financial performance, as well as other developments within the company (e.g., a change in the management of the company can have a positive or negative effect on the share's price)

- how successful the industry in which that company operates is overall

- the stability of the country (financially and politically) in which the shares are traded

- the stability of the industry and the impact of other countries' political and financial circumstances on that industry.

A lot of detailed analysis goes into trying to predict which shares will do well. The people who do *fundamental* analysis carefully study particular industry groups and are often in frequent contact with the management of the companies they watch. Since the performance of a company's stock is closely related to that company's earnings, fundamental analysis focuses on estimating what those earnings will be over the next one or two years, as well as the company's standing in the industry and how the industry as a whole is performing. While fundamental analysis focuses on the performance of the company, another form of analysis — *technical* analysis — focuses on how the shares themselves are increasing or decreasing in value. Technical analysis is based on the idea that the price patterns of individual stocks — and of the stock market generally — tend to repeat themselves. Technical analysts focus on compiling and analysing past trends in prices and volume. The problem with using only technical analysis is that while a trend may be up for the industry as a whole, the performance of an individual stock may not mirror the projected positive performance.

In trying to determine the best stocks to buy, and the right time to buy, institutional investors rely heavily on the information provided by both fundamental and technical analysts. But much of the information generated seems like Greek to the rest of us. That's one reason we tend to rely heavily on the advice we receive from people who are in the know. For some, picking individual stocks can seem a bit like throwing a dart at a board and hoping for the best. Of course, the more you know about the stock you are investing in, the less random the throw and the closer to the bull's-eye you'll be. That's why it's so important to take the gamble out of investing by using all the resources available to become informed.

While people talk of "playing the stock market," investing isn't a game. Remember rule number 1: Make sure you know what you're buying before you buy.

MONEY LESSON

(AGE 11+)

In deciding which stocks to buy, your first step should be to ask your child to describe the products and services she uses. List those products on a piece of paper.

You may have to do a bit of prompting. Here are some ideas:

- What types of foods (soda, cereal, chips) do you like?
- What games do you like best?
- What stores do you shop in for clothing, shoes?
- What movie studios make the movies you enjoy the most?
- What are your favourite restaurants?

The next step is to list the companies that make those products or provide those services. Some of these companies will be traded on a stock exchange while others may be traded over-the-counter. Have your child write to those companies and ask for their annual reports. This will show her how much the company earned last year so she can see if the company is getting stronger. She can see what the company has paid out in dividends and how this compares to the dividends paid by companies making similar products.

WHAT EXACTLY IS THE STOCK MARKET?

Just as foreign currency can be bought and sold on the foreign exchange market, so too can stocks be bought and sold on the stock market. The term "stock market" refers to the organized trading of stocks, including trading on stock exchanges. There are many active exchanges around the world that are used for trading (buying and selling) stocks. Here are a few examples:

- In Canada: Alberta, Montreal, Quebec, Toronto, Vancouver and Winnipeg.

- In the U.S.: the American, Boston, Chicago, Cincinnati, Detroit, Midwest, National, New York, Pacific, Pittsburg, Salt Lake, Philadelphia-Baltimore-Washington, Spokane and NASDAQ.

- In Europe: Amsterdam, Brussels, Frankfurt, London, Madrid, Milan, Paris and Zurich.

- Elsewhere: Australia, Tokyo, Hong Kong, Mexico, New Zealand and Singapore.

These exchanges are organized and regulated based on the laws in effect in the countries where they're located. Almost every developed country has at least one stock exchange, and there are over 200 exchanges around the world.

To trade on the floor of a stock exchange, you must be a member of that exchange. This is referred to as buying a seat on the exchange. These seats trade much like stocks, being bought and sold based on demand. In 1987, when the market was hot and there was much money to be made, a seat on the New York Stock Exhange sold for $1.2 million. However, in 1990, when the market cooled substantially, seats sold for $400,000.

Companies often choose to become listed on a stock exchange because of the prestige and high profile such a listing brings. Listing a company's shares also makes it easier to determine the value of the company (called its market capitalization).

Companies not listed on an exchange may still be accessible to investors. While listed stocks trade in a specific location at a specific time each day, unlisted or over-the-counter stocks are traded through a wide communication network, which links hundreds of brokers and dealers. Unlisted exchanges have no fixed trading hours and sometimes trade 24 hours a day. The over-the-counter market in the U.S. is huge, while in Canada it is relatively small.

HOW TO READ THE STOCK PAGES

When you first look at the stock pages, the numbers and abbreviations can be confusing. Over time, once your eyes become used to the jumble of fractions and letters, you will be able to find things quickly.

Every stock quotation is made up of a bid and an asked price. The bid is the highest price a buyer is willing to pay for a share, and the asked price (sometime called the "offer") is the lowest price any seller is willing to accept. When a share is bought or sold, it is usually at one of these prices or somewhere in between.

This is what a stock list looks like in the newspaper.

52-Week					Yield						
High / Low		Stock	Sym	Div	%	PE	High	Low	Close	Chg	Vol
$57\frac{1}{8}$	$47\frac{1}{4}$	AT&T	T	1.32	2.6	16.4	$50\frac{7}{8}$	$50\frac{1}{4}$	$50\frac{3}{8}$	$-\frac{3}{8}$	12869
$59\frac{3}{8}$	$39\frac{1}{8}$	CocaCola	KO	.88	1.5	27.8	58	$57\frac{5}{8}$	$57\frac{3}{4}$	$-\frac{3}{8}$	12407

And here is the information each of the columns provides:

1. 52-Week High/Low: The highest and lowest price of the stock over the past 52 weeks.

2. Stock: The name of the company listed.

3. Sym: The symbol used for the stock.

4. Div: Cash dividend per share, shown in dollars and cents. In the case of AT&T, shareholders would receive $1.32 for each share held. Generally dividends are paid quarterly in four equal instalments. So, in the case of CocaCola, you would receive 22 cents per share for each share you held in four quarterly instalments.

5. Yield %: Percent yield is one way of expressing the stock's current value. It indicates how much dividend is given relative to the price paid for the stock. You arrive at this percentage amount by dividing the dividend by the closing price (close) for the stock. In the case of CocaCola, for example, the dividend of 88 cents divided by the close price of $57.75 and multiplied by 100 to arrive at a yield of 1.5 percent.

7. PE: This is the abbreviation for price/earnings ratio. It refers to the relationship between the cost of one share and the yearly earnings of the company. This can be a useful tool in assessing whether a stock is over- or under-valued. However, you cannot use only PE when comparing stocks, since a low PE doesn't necessarily mean value. And PE ratios can be affected by how much demand there is for a particular stock. Rather, the PE should be used in comparing a stock's current performance with its past performance. It can also be useful in comparing companies that are in the same business.

8. High: The highest price offered for a share.

9. Low: The lowest price offered for a share.

10. Close: The price of the share when the market closed.

11. Chg: This is the net change, which compares the closing price with the closing price from the previous day's trading.

12. Vol: This shows the volume of shares traded on the previous trading day and is abbreviated. To determine the actual number of shares traded, you

must multiply the number shown by 100. So, assuming this is today's listing, then yesterday, 1,286,900 shares of AT&T were traded.

MONEY LESSON

(AGE 11+)

You don't actually have to buy stock to become familiar with investing. You can also make a game of investing. When there's no real money on the line, losing can be a lot less painful.

Begin by setting a specific amount of money you'll invest — say $10,000. Your objective is to see how much you can increase your investment dollars through smart investing.

Choose five or six stocks that both you and your child are interested in. Do all your homework — that's part of choosing the stocks — in terms of finding out as much as possible about those stocks. Make a chart for each of the stocks you have pretended to buy.

Show your child how to find these stocks listed in the business section of the newspaper and how to read the information in the stock charts. Record how your stocks are doing each month. Remember, to make a profit on your fictitious portfolio, at some point you will have to sell your stock and buy other stock. While this game can go on forever, consider setting a specific time frame — perhaps a school year — for reporting on your investment portfolio.

Eventually you should reach the point where you and your child feel comfortable actually getting into the market by buying some of the shares you have been tracking.

If stock-picking becomes a favourite activity in your house, then I strongly recommend you take the time to learn how to analyse stocks. Your local shareholders' association or investment club will be able to direct you to a good source of information.

Even when a stock comes highly recommended by an investment adviser, it's a good idea for you and your child to do some research of your own to make sure you know what you're getting into. Once you've chosen a stock you feel may be a good buy, research the following:

Qualitative Factors
• the potential market for the product or service
• the competition
• the company's management abilities.

Quantitative Factors
• how has the company has performed year after year (referred to in the industry as "year-over-year" results) on
  - earnings
  - revenues
  - cash flow
  - debt
  - sales

Of course, the basis for sound analysis rests with knowing what to look for. After all, without a road map, the numbers may seem pretty confusing. Learning how to analyse stocks is just the ticket for unravelling the mysteries of qualitative and quantitative analysis.

KNOW THE RISKS

Often when I speak with individuals about investing and introduce the idea of using stocks, the reaction I get is quite strong, "Oh no, I couldn't invest in the stock market. It's much too risky!" Many people are concerned with keeping their money safe. They want to preserve their initial investment, or capital, so that it does not decrease in value. There are two types of capital preservation: nominal and real. Nominal preservation simply means keeping the dollar value of the investment intact. In other words, if you start out with $10,000, you want to make sure that at the end of the day you still have at least $10,000. Real preservation means protecting the purchasing power of the investment against inflation. To preserve or increase the purchasing power of any investment, some level of risk must be taken.

When looking at the issue of safety, view it from three perspectives:

1. The level of *volatility* associated with the investment. In other words, how much the investment's value will fluctuate over the short term.

2. The level of *risk* associated with the investment, or the potential for losing the original capital investment.

3. Your emotional safety needs or *investment personality*, or how much sleep you'll lose worrying about your investments' short-term behaviour.

TAKE THIS TEST

Most people aren't aware of their investment personality and how it affects, or should affect, their investment choices. On the following page is a short test that will help you (or your child) determine what your investment personality is like and how that will affect on your investment choices. Following the test is a short explanation of what the numbers mean.

On page 164 is another test that will help you compare how you think you are (that is, the types of investments you think you would buy) versus how you have traditionally invested.

INVESTOR, KNOW THYSELF

Circle the number that best applies to you.

	Not at all		Yes, definitely

1. I am willing to accept some fluctuation in the value of my investments for the potential of capital growth and high returns.　1　2　3　4　5

2. Day-by-day price changes in my investment don't bother me. I'm investing for the long term (more than ten years).　1　2　3　4　5

3. My investment income is surplus to my current needs. I don't need it to pay my living expenses.　1　2　3　4　5

4. I have enough money set aside for emergencies. I'd like to know how to make the rest grow a lot more.　1　2　3　4　5

5. I follow the financial markets regularly.　1　2　3　4　5

6. I am as comfortable investing in the stock market or in equity mutual funds as I am in income-bearing investments.　1　2　3　4　5

WHAT THE NUMBERS MEAN

If you selected mostly 1's and 2's, you are an income-oriented investor. Your main investment goal is to generate income through interest or dividends. You place a lot of emphasis on the safety of your capital and the security of a fixed return.

If you selected mostly 3's, you are a balanced investor. You want to achieve a balance; you want to maintain an even approach between earning capital gains and earning a higher income through interest or dividends. You are right in the middle in terms of emphasizing security of income. You are willing to accept some fluctuation in the value of your portfolio in order to earn higher capital gains.

If you selected mostly 4's and 5's, you are a growth-oriented investor. Your objective is to earn a high level of growth. You want to emphasize equities to generate medium- to long-term higher rates of return. You are less interested in interest or dividend income, and are prepared to accept a greater level of fluctuation in the value of your investment portfolio.

How well did you know your own investment-risk profile? Many people think they know themselves well. Others may never have thought about how they handle the issue of risk and how important safety is to them. Still others may, in fact, hold one perception of themselves ("I am a growth-oriented investor") while their behaviour — the actual investments they choose to buy — indicates something quite different.

On the following page is another short test. Complete this test now, and then look at how your *actual* investment personality (based on the types of investments you now hold) compares to your *perceived* investment personality. You may be surprised at the difference.

Understanding and being true to your investment personality is an important part of making the right investment decisions. As investors, we have to learn to deal with the ups and downs of investing. So too, must we help our children understand and learn to deal with the risk of loss and the need to keep a sense of proportion when they have a string of wins.

I have heard hundreds of stories about people who jumped into investments with which they weren't really comfortable because their friends had them, or because they were being strongly promoted by influential financial advisers. If those people had first taken the time to know themselves in terms of their

163

HOW WELL DO YOU
REALLY KNOW YOURSELF?

Circle the number that best applies to you.

	Not at all			Yes, definitely

1. The investments I have fluctuate in value.　　　1　2　3　4　5

2. I have no trouble sleeping at night even
when the value of my investments falls
significantly.　　　1　2　3　4　5

3. I don't use my investment income to supplement
my day-to-day needs.　　　1　2　3　4　5

4. I already have enough money set aside for
emergencies (minimum 3 months' income).　　　1　2　3　4　5

5. I read the financial papers at least two to three
times a week.　　　1　2　3　4　5

6. I hold as many equity investments as I do interest-
bearing investments.　　　1　2　3　4　5

---

personal investment comfort zone, there'd have been a lot less panic when the investments faltered or when the returns generated did not immediately meet expectations.

In general, whenever you wish to increase the potential return on your investment, you must give up a proportionate amount of safety. While investing in the stock market does carry risk, by being aware of the things that may affect your investments, you can make informed decisions that reduce those risks.

Risk can be described as the possibility of loss occurring. There are two basic types of risks: systematic, which affects the prices of all investments; and unsystematic, which is unique to a company or industry.

164

SYSTEMATIC RISK INCLUDES:

- *Market Risk.* This refers to uncertainty about future price of an investment because of changing economic conditions or unpredictable changes in investor attitudes. For example, the announcement by the federal government regarding lower-than-expected economic growth often results in a broad decline in share prices as investors lower their expectations of corporate earnings. Grave illness or assassination of a political figure can affect the general market, as well. Common shares and real estate are extremely vulnerable to market risk.

- *Purchasing-Power Risk.* This reflects the uncertainty about the purchasing power of investments because of changes in the rate of inflation. Investors who stick their money in their mattresses or choose the safety of savings accounts find that over time their money buys less. Investments such as common shares, equity mutual funds and real estate have, traditionally, been valuable for minimizing purchasing power risk. The true test of how well you are beating purchasing-power risk is your real rate of return.

- *Interest-Rate Risk.* This refers to the uncertainty of future prices and returns on investments because of changes in interest rates. If interest rates rise, bond prices fall, and if interest rates fall, bond prices rise. The investor who holds a long-term bond during a period of rising interest rates will see the value of the bond decline. As mentioned in the previous chapter, contrary to popular belief, there is a level of risk associated with even the safest of investments: certificates of deposit. The risk is that interest rates will rise and you will be locked in to a lower rate. Alternatively, if you've invested at a high rate, the risk is then that interest rates will be significantly lower when it comes time to renew. Certificates with terms less than one year, treasury bills, and bonds with a variable (or floating) interest rate have a low level of interest-rate risk. Long-term bonds, mortgages and three- to five-year certificates of deposits are all vulnerable to interest-rate risk.

- *Political Risk.* This refers to the adverse impact a change in government policy, sometimes due to the defeat of the incumbent party, has on security prices and returns. These types of policy changes include the imposition of price and wage controls, reduction in subsidy grants, tax increases and restrictive tariffs.

UNSYSTEMATIC RISK INCLUDES:

- *Business Risk.* Unlike the four forms of systematic risk, business risk is unique to each individual company. Adverse factors such as the loss of a major contract, a strike, new antipollution regulations or the loss of a key executive, may negatively affect a company's earnings. The change in earnings may result in a decline in the stock's price. Many of these changes are temporary. However, if the decline is of a permanent nature, the loss in value would result in a capital loss to the investor. The more volatile or changeable the earning stream of a company, the greater the degree of business risk. Common shares are particularly vulnerable to business risk.

- *Default (or Credit) Risk.* This refers to the danger that the issuer will be unable to meet its interest or principal payments or other financial obligations due to a decline in earnings. For example, a high-quality corporation with a $10,000,000 bond issue outstanding on which it pays $1,000,000 in interest might encounter financial difficulties due to a loss of market share for its product. The credit rating given to debt investments such as bonds indicates the level of credit risk associated with the investment.

DIVERSIFICATION

To balance your investment portfolio, you need to diversify your investments, that is, spread your investment dollars over more than one type of investment. Remember the old rule about not putting all your eggs in one basket? The reason diversification — or asset mix — is important is that by purchasing several different investments, you can reduce your exposure to investment risk. If one investment doesn't do particularly well, others may make up the difference.

Your investment portfolio can be diversified in a variety of ways:

- by the types of investments — using bonds, deposits, stocks, mutual funds and real estate

- by the quality of the investments

- by region (in Canada, North America, globally)

by currency

by levels of liquidity, holding some long-term deposits such as stripped bonds or equity funds, along with some shorter-term investments such as treasury bills

One misconception is that if you buy stock of several different companies, you will be automatically well diversified. This isn't necessarily so. To effectively diversify, not only do you have to buy stocks of different companies, but also within different industries and across different countries.

INVESTMENT TIME HORIZON

One final consideration is your investment time horizon, or how long you plan to keep the investment.

Short-term investors — those investing for up to five years or less — should avoid putting the majority of their money in equity investments where the risk of losing that money is greater. Choosing fixed-income investments that generate a steady return while offering a higher level of security is a better idea for these investors.

Medium-term investors — those who plan to keep their investments for five to ten years — should balance their investment dollars using both equity and fixed-income alternatives. Or they might invest in an alternative that offers built-in diversification, such as a balanced mutual fund.

Long-term investors — those with a time horizon of ten years or more — would be wise to choose an asset mix that is weighted more heavily with growth (or equity) investments. Since equities have historically outperformed all other types of investments over the long term, people with an investment horizon of ten years or more should be primarily invested in equities.

Again, the proviso to all this is that you have to buy investments with which you're comfortable. You may have a long-term investment horizon, but if you're uncomfortable with the thought of your investment fluctuating in value, you may not be an equity investor.

Since no single investment offers the perfect opportunity for the highest return, full liquidity, most security, greatest tax advantages, income generation and convenience, you need to keep your specific goals and investment

167

objectives clearly in mind. And as you get older, or as your personal circumstances or economic conditions change, so too must the individual investments held if you wish to maintain a well-diversified investment portfolio.

Not everyone is cut out to be a stock-market investor. As you have probably gathered, to do it right takes time and energy. You have to be vigilant about keeping current on what's happening in the economy, as well as what's happening in the company you've bought shares in. If you find all this too much work for you, there are alternatives, and you can read all about them in chapter 11.

11 THE WORLD OF MUTUAL FUNDS

One of the best ways to get into investing without scads of cash is through mutual funds. Because they are very accessible and professionally managed, mutual funds take much of the work out of investing. And because of the diversification they offer, they also can reduce much of the risk associated with buying individual shares.

This chapter presents a detailed overview of mutual funds and how they can be used to begin an investment portfolio. Depending on your child's age and interest, you can read through the material and introduce the concepts a bit at a time, or you can simply hand him this chapter and discuss it with him later.

The exercises in the previous chapter translate easily to the area of mutual funds. For example, the exercise on page 153 can easily be done using mutual funds investments instead of individual stocks.

WELCOME TO THE WORLD OF MUTUAL FUNDS

Mutual funds date back to the 1800s when a Scottish and English investment trust sold shares to investors. Mutual funds sprung up in the U.S. in 1924, and in Canada in the 1930s. Today, trillions of dollars are invested in mutual funds.

In the past few years, mutual funds have become increasingly popular. One reason is that mutual funds have consistently outperformed traditional investments such as savings accounts and certificates of deposit. Another is that mutual-fund sellers have used these very accessible investment alternatives to attract investors with smaller amounts of investment dollars. Aggressive marketing has increased our focus on this product as the seemingly constant arrival of new funds in the marketplace, and the accompanying advertising and media coverage, has increased our awareness. As people become more sophisticated in managing their money, and as our expectations of how our investments should perform rise, we have become more and more enthralled with mutual funds.

WHAT EXACTLY IS A MUTUAL FUND?

A mutual fund is a pool of money gathered from thousands of investors and invested in a large diversified portfolio of investments. Mutual funds are managed by professionals, so as an investor, you do not have to be concerned with any investment decision other than the initial decision of which fund to purchase (and, of course, when to sell).

Fund managers buy and sell investments in the mutual funds (that is, the underlying stocks, bonds or mortgages), and the investors share in the growth and income generated by the fund. In effect, a mutual fund is owned by the people who have invested in it. Since all the money is pooled together, invested and managed by professionals, mutual funds are sometimes called "pooled," "investment" or "managed" funds.

WHY WOULD I BUY A MUTUAL FUND?

Do you find the concept of investing a little frightening? Many people do. That's why they stick with traditional "safe" alternatives like certificates of deposit. But by staying with these tried-and-true investments, you may be doing yourself a disservice in terms of the return you're earning. Using mutual funds, you can enter a new world of investing, one that offers the potential for higher return. And because there are almost as many different mutual funds as there are investment objectives, you can choose the funds that best meet your personal safety needs.

Here are some reasons mutual funds are attractive investment alternatives:

- Professional management. Most of us don't have the experience, training or time to be able to select investments and know when to buy and sell those investments to make a profit. Since mutual funds are professionally managed, you don't have to be concerned with the day-to-day decisions required to ensure your investment performs well. Knowledgeable professionals with years of experience do the work for you.

- Investment diversification. It has been estimated that if you are investing in individual securities, you'll need at least $150,000 to achieve a reasonable level of diversification. Mutual funds, however, let you achieve a satisfactory level of diversification with an investment as small as $100. Mutual funds typically hold a wide variety of investments spread over many instruments, so your return won't be adversely affected by the poor performance of any one investment.

For example, if you invest $3,000 in an individual stock that sells for $10 a share, you'll own 300 shares. If the price of that stock falls to $8 a share, then your initial investment would be worth only $2,400. That's a loss of $600, or 20 percent of the original investment. And that loss can come very quickly. Individual stocks can fluctuate substantially over short periods of time because of market changes influenced by economic or political events. On the other hand, an investment of $3,000 in an equity mutual fund would purchase units of a fund that had invested in the shares of dozens of different companies. The individual performance of any one company's shares would not have a severe negative effect on the overall unit value of the mutual fund. Because of this diversification, your exposure to risk is significantly reduced, and therefore, the potential loss of your initial investment is significantly reduced.

- Accessibility. Since many mutual-fund accounts can be opened with as little as $100, mutual funds are extremely accessible and have allowed a lot more people to enter the world of investing. Mutual funds are easy to buy and easy to sell, and that makes them a very convenient investment. Many mutual-fund companies also offer preauthorized purchase plans, and most offer automatic reinvestment of income, referred to as dividend reinvestment programs, or DRIPs.

- Liquidity. One of the aspects that affects our decisions to invest is the access we will have to our money in the event that we need it quickly. Everyone should have some cash readily available to meet emergency expenses. You might also want to be fairly liquid so that you will be able to quickly move your money into other investments as opportunities arise. Most mutual funds have a fairly high level of liquidity, which means you can cash in on short notice.

- Wide choice of options. People often associate mutual funds with equity funds, but in fact, there are many more types of funds from which to choose. Mutual funds provide options ranging from investment in stocks, to investment in bonds and mortgages, to investment in money-market vehicles such as treasury bills. You can invest in North American–based funds or in international funds that allow you to take advantage of the growth in the global economy. You can even invest in industry-specific funds that focus on industries such as precious metals, energy, communications and the like. And with mutual funds, you can choose the types of investments that not only provide the return you seek, but may also satisfy your need for special tax treatment.

- Potentially higher returns. Mutual funds offer you the opportunity to enter the investment marketplace to earn potentially higher returns than can be achieved with traditional investments such as certificates. The trick to using mutual funds successfully is know what you're buying before you buy, and know what factors will affect your fund's performance so that you can build an investment portfolio with an asset mix that's right for you.

HOW MUTUAL FUNDS WORK

When you buy a mutual fund, your money is converted into "units." Each unit represents a portion of the mutual fund's total assets. For example, if the current unit value of a mutual fund is $12 and you wish to invest $600, you'd be able to purchase 50 units of the fund.

The unit price of a mutual fund generally depends on the current market price of the underlying investments, such as stocks and bonds. (The only exception to this is a money-market fund the unit value of which is usually fixed.) When the mutual-fund holdings change value, the value of the units also changes.

Mutual funds should be considered medium- to long-term investments, because unit values may go up or down in the short term. However, in the long run, mutual funds are managed to provide superior gains over time.

A lower unit value can even work to your advantage if the income generated is being reinvested or if you are taking advantage of dollar-cost averaging by making periodic purchases over the long term. The lower the unit price, the greater the number of units that can be purchased. Naturally it is always in your interest to "buy low and sell high." That's the objective of any investment: to make a profit.

WHAT IS DOLLAR-COST AVERAGING?

Dollar-cost averaging is a complex name for a simple investment technique. Rather than accumulating a large sum of money before making an investment, you are wiser to invest small amounts at regular intervals.

Let's say the unit value of a particular mutual fund fluctuated as follows over a 12-month period:

	Unit Value
January	$12.00
February	$13.20
March	$13.40
April	$9.50
May	$9.40
June	$8.60
July	$9.70
August	$10.25
September	$9.35
October	$10.50
November	$12.20
December	$13.00

If you saved $80 a month and invested $960 in this fund in December, you would be paying $13 per unit and could therefore buy 73.8 units.

However, if you *invested* $80 a month, here's how your acquisitions would look:

	Unit Value	Units Purchased
January	$12.00	6.66
February	$13.20	6.06
March	$13.40	5.97
April	$9.50	8.42
May	$9.40	8.51
June	$8.60	9.30
July	$9.70	8.24
August	$10.25	7.80
September	$9.35	8.55
October	$10.50	7.61
November	$12.20	6.55
December	$13.00	6.15

By using the principles of dollar-cost averaging, you'd be able to buy 89.96 units for an average price of $10.92. So by making purchases at regular intervals, you would have 17 units more than if you made your total purchase in December. At December's unit price, that's a return of $221 on an initial investment of $960. Pretty good, isn't it? The key is this: the average purchase price is less than market average because you buy more units at a lower price.

Dollar-cost averaging means you don't have to worry about investing at the right time. However, for it to work effectively, you should use it as a long-term strategy — and stick with it! Don't let market performance shake your trust. It's a great system.

CONSIDER BEFORE YOU BUY

- Know what you're buying before you buy. If I'm beginning to sound like a broken record, it's because this is the most important rule in investing and I can't stress it enough. Although every piece of advertising clearly states that a mutual fund's past performance is no predictor of future performance, virtually all investors pick funds based on how they have performed most recently. This is a mistake. Last year's biggest winners are often not the big winners this year. And if you bought last year's champion, you may have to sit through a year or two of lacklustre performance before things pick up again.

- Don't be greedy. Typically, very high rates of return are associated with the more volatile funds. Rather than allowing yourself to be intrigued by a promise of 25, 30 or 40 percent returns, decide what you can live with, relative to inflation and other investment returns, and then look for an investment with a long-term track record of consistent performance. Compare any fund you're considering with other funds in the same group or sector. There's no point in comparing the ABC Gold Fund with the XYZ Pharmaceutical Fund.

- Your mutual-fund purchase should fit in with the other investments you've made. Once you've determined the investment mix appropriate for you, stick with it.

- Long-term results are the key to analysing a mutual fund's performance. Over the short term, almost every mutual fund can claim amazing results — but over the long term, only the best-managed funds stand out. Don't look simply at the average rate of return; you need to see how the fund has performed each year to see whether or not it has consistently met its objectives, so ask to see the fund's year-over-year returns.

- Ask how long the fund manager has been with the fund. A mutual fund is only as good as its management. If the fund manager has changed recently, wait a while before you buy to see how the fund performs under the new manager. That doesn't mean that if the fund management has changed, you should immediately jump out of the fund. However, it does mean that you should pay close attention to the fund's performance. All else being equal, the performance shouldn't change. If it does, then it may be time to change.

- Minimize the costs of changing your investments by choosing a good fund "family." Many mutual-fund companies sell several different types of funds under the same brand (or family) name. Most fund families allow you to switch from one fund to another without cost so that you can adjust your asset mix as your needs — and economic circumstances — change.

- Look at the real return (the stated return less any commission charged by the fund) generated by the fund before you make a decision. There are plenty of funds out there; some charge a commission and others don't. While you won't pick a mutual fund simply because it is no-load (that is, no commission charged), you should consider the cost, over the long term, in paying a load. Take the time to calculate the real return once the commission is accounted for.

Allow a reasonable amount of time for funds to perform. And once you've bought with a specific time frame in mind, stick to your guns. I often meet people who have bought equity funds that may not be performing to their expectations. They may have held the fund only for one or two years, but are seriously considering selling and getting into something else. I'll tell you what I've told them.

Since you've purchased an equity fund (which is considered a long-term investment), you need to give the fund enough time to perform. These funds aren't designed to give you an overnight million — despite the advertised spectacular returns. Rather, equity funds are designed to outperform other types of mutual funds over the long term — that's over a ten-year horizon. If you don't have ten years, stay out of this type of investment.

"But what about the loss I've taken?" they often ask. Well, the fact is if you buy a mutual fund that goes down in value, you haven't lost anything until you sell it. It's the selling of the fund that creates the loss. If you hold the fund and it goes up again, you may break even or make a profit.

Of course, there may be times when a fund just isn't worth holding. You may be stuck with a rotten fund manager, or the industry you invested in may have completely bottomed out. Once you've decided that a fund isn't going to perform over the long term, then you should cut your losses and get into something that will put your money to work for you.

Just because you've finally taken the plunge and invested in a mutual fund doesn't mean you can never go back. If interest rates rise to a level you're comfortable with, you can always switch back to a certificate of deposit. You can't beat it for security, providing the real return (taking inflation into account) meets your investment objectives.

In the meantime, widen your perspective a little. Learn all about mutual funds in general, and how diversification can help you achieve your objectives. Call the individual mutual-fund companies you're interested in and get information on the year-over-year performance of the fund, as well as the fund manager's track record. Investigate your options and look for new opportunities.

TYPES OF MUTUAL FUNDS

There are hundreds of different mutual funds currently available. These funds purchase different types of investments to meet each fund's specific objectives. While they all operate more or less in the same way, their investment portfolios are different.

Here are the general types of funds available:

MONEY-MARKET FUNDS

Money-market funds invest in money-market instruments such as short-term government bonds, treasury bills, term deposits, certificates, short-term promissory notes and banker's acceptances. They provide high levels of interest income with very little risk to your capital.

Money-market funds differ from other types of mutual funds in the way their unit values are set. While the unit values of other mutual funds fluctuate, rising or falling, to provide you with a capital gain or capital loss, the unit value of a money-market fund remains fairly constant. The return provided by a money-market fund is the income that is paid. Since the unit value seldom fluctuates, there is little possibility that you will lose your initial investment. This is one reason money-market funds are so popular.

Money-market funds offer you the opportunity to take advantage of investments that typically are not available to individual investors or that require large amounts of money. You can also benefit from the economies of scale associated with a mutual fund making the purchase. When purchasing treasury bills, for example, the price quoted (described in terms of the return, or yield, you will earn) will vary; the more you invest, the better the price you'll be quoted. Since mutual funds can buy treasury bills in large quantities, unit holders can earn a higher return (because prices quoted are more favourable for large transactions) than if they tried to buy treasury bills directly.

FIXED-INCOME FUNDS

Fixed-income funds may invest in portfolios of mortgages, bonds or preferred shares. Since the interest on a bond, a mortgage or a dividend on a preferred share is established at the time it's issued, it's referred to as a fixed-income investment.

The main objective of a *dividend* income fund is the generation of regular income in the form of dividends. Most of these funds invest in preferred shares, while some invest in a combination of high-quality common shares, as well as holding preferred shares in the portfolio.

Mortgage funds hold a portfolio of mortgages, usually first mortgages on residential properties since they are more secure. Fund managers may have a mix of term lengths in the portfolio. They try to vary the mix to take advantage of interest-rate trends and invest in a variety of geographical areas. The primary form of return is interest income, with some capital gains possible.

Bond funds hold a combination of bonds — from corporate- to government-issued — in their portfolios. The interest rates of the assets of the fund do not change even if current interest rates change. However, that does not mean that the fund always provides the same rate of income. Fund managers are regularly buying and selling the investments in the fund to secure maximum income while preserving capital. Bond funds also offer the potential of capital gains.

Preferred-share funds are usually classified as fixed-income funds. While they represent equity in a company, their primary objective is to provide an income through the dividends they pay.

Fixed-income funds are more stable than equity (or growth) funds. However, the long-term rates of return on fixed-income funds tend to be more modest than those of equity-based funds.

BALANCED FUNDS

The objective of a balanced fund is to achieve both income and capital appreciation. Such a fund has a mixture of equity, fixed-income and liquid investments. The equity investments provide the opportunity for growth while the fixed-income and liquid investments provide regular income. Preferred shares are sometimes included to provide additional income.

Balanced funds are the most highly diversified because their assets are so widely spread. Fund managers vary the balance between equity and fixed-income investments depending on market conditions. For example, in a period of declining equity/stock market conditions, a balanced fund will likely concentrate the majority of its investments in fixed-income securities. If stock-market conditions are strong, the fund will invest in more equities. The result is reduced risk.

A new variation on this theme is the asset-allocation fund. Asset allocation is the latest investment fad and refers to the balancing of volatility and risk with the desire for increased return (sounds like a balanced fund, doesn't it?).

GROWTH FUNDS

Growth funds invest in stocks or common shares of companies and are often referred to as equity funds. When you purchase a growth fund, you're usually hoping for a significant increase in the value of your investment over the long term. If the unit value goes up and you sell some or all of your units, you'll realize a capital gain. However, if the unit value goes down and you sell some or all of your units, you'll have a capital loss.

Equity funds vary in growth potential and in risk, depending on the specific assets held in their portfolios. They buy shares in stock markets within their own country and around the world. Their unit values are affected by the relative value of the individual shares on the stock exchange, as well as the current strength of currency in which they are denominated. In fact, foreign

179

stocks can be a good investment just because their value may increase due to changes in exchange rates.

INTERNATIONAL FUNDS

Some funds invest in securities from a number of different countries or regions of the world to take advantage of different economic conditions. While conditions in one country may be poor, the situation in another may be very healthy. Therefore, these funds concentrate on taking advantage of the global economy. Fund managers work to earn the highest returns possible by diversifying across global markets. When making their decisions, they must also take into account changes in exchange rates.

REAL ESTATE FUNDS

Real estate funds invest in income-generating commercial and industrial properties. Your return is based on the income the properties produce, as well as any capital gains when properties are sold. Real estate funds' unit values are based on the market value of real estate held. Appraisals on the properties held by the fund are done at least once a year, sometimes more frequently, and the unit values are adjusted accordingly. For this reason, real estate funds can be far less liquid than most other forms of mutual funds, the units of which are usually valued daily or weekly. Therefore, this type of mutual fund should only be considered as a long-term investment.

INDEXED FUNDS

Indexed funds are funds that are, for the most part, managed by a computer. They are designed to duplicate an underlying index, such as the Standard & Poor's 500 Index. Unlike other mutual funds where individuals or teams search high and low for just the right investments, an indexed-fund manager simply invests to match the performance of the index to which it is tied. The advantage of an indexed fund is that you're guaranteed to do as well as the market does. Also, because there's no research required and few transaction fees, the management fees are much lower.

SPECIALTY FUNDS

Specialty funds tend to concentrate their assets in one particular sector of the economy or in one specific country. Some specialize in energy, high technology, telecommunications, pharmaceuticals or precious metals. Others specialize in one country such as Japan or Germany, or in a region such as Asia or Europe. Returns on specialized funds tend to fluctuate considerably from one year to the next. They have the potential for very high capital appreciation, but can also be extremely risky. Therefore, these types of funds should only be used as long-term investments.

SOCIALLY CONSCIOUS FUNDS

If you're concerned about investing in companies engaged in business that is socially unattractive or that you consider unethical, this type of fund may be just the ticket. These funds have chosen to exclude stocks that do not fit with their social consciences. For example, a green fund would look not only at a company's financial performance, but also at how environmentally conscious it is. Some ethical funds exclude companies involved in the manufacture of weapons or cigarettes, while others exclude companies who trade with countries known for human rights violations.

HOW INTEREST RATE CHANGES AFFECT MUTUAL FUND PERFORMANCE

Depending on the assets held, mutual funds can be affected by changes in interest rates. Fixed-income funds (mortgage and bond funds) are "interest sensitive." Generally, when interest rates go up, the unit values of the interest-sensitive funds will likely decrease. For example, if you buy a bond that pays six percent interest, it gives you a $30 return on a $500 investment. If interest rates go up, the bond is considered less valuable because new bonds are offering a higher rate of interest (more than the six percent being paid on your bond). The reverse is also true: when interest rates go down, the investment is worth more.

181

Similarly, if you hold a mortgage at ten percent and interest rates go down, the mortgage is considered more valuable because new mortgages are offering a lower return. Since these funds are interest sensitive, both the yield and unit price fluctuate based on changes in interest rates.

Bond funds tend to be more interest sensitive than mortgage funds. That's because the longer the term to maturity, the more impact changes in rates have on an investment — rates on longer-term instruments tend to be more volatile than shorter-term rates. Bond funds may hold bonds that do not mature for ten or 15 years. On the other hand, the maximum term for a mortgage is usually five years. As a result, bond funds react more strongly to changes in interest rates than do mortgage funds.

THE PROSPECTUS & ANNUAL REPORT

Legally, mutual-fund sellers are required to provide you with a copy of the prospectus before you buy. This document contains information about:

- the fund's investment objectives, policies and restrictions
- the people responsible for the management of the fund and its assets
- how income is distributed
- costs charged to the fund
- the purchaser's statutory rights
- taxation issues
- risk factors

Mutual funds also produce annual reports that review how their funds have performed and provide details on the specific investments held.

Make sure you read the prospectus and most recent annual report before you buy a fund. I've heard dozens of stories from people who felt they were sold a bill of goods. Had they taken the time to read the prospectus, they would likely have come up with quite a few questions before they were ready to put their money on the table. As an investor it is your responsibility to buy the right investments for your needs. Blaming a salesperson for putting you into an investment that you didn't understand is a cop-out. Do your homework. Know what you're buying before you buy.

VALUATION DATE

The valuation date is the date the value of the fund is established. Many funds are valued weekly on the last business day of the week. Others are valued each business day.

On the valuation date, the net asset value (NAV) of the units is set. The NAV of the units is equal to the NAV of the total fund divided by the total units outstanding.

WHAT DOES IT COST TO BUY A MUTUAL FUND?

There are a variety of costs associated with purchasing, holding and selling mutual funds. Not all funds levy the same types of charges, nor do they all charge the same fees for similar services.

A number of mutual funds charge a sales fee — also called a "commission," "acquisition fee" or "load" — on the sale of units of their funds. This acquisition fee is referred to by a number of different names, depending on when it is charged. Some funds have an initial sales charge — called a front-end load, or an "in" — which is charged on the amount originally invested. This fee can be as high as nine percent and is usually negotiable, depending on the amount being invested. Some funds charge a redemption fee — referred to as a back-end load, or an "out" — and this is payable when the units of a fund are redeemed, or sold.

A redemption fee may be calculated on the initial purchase cost, or it may be calculated on the value of the investment when it is sold, which, of course, may be much higher. However, most redemption fees are usually designed to reduce to zero after the fund has been held for a specific number of years, typically five to six years. That's one good reason a mutual fund should be viewed as a long-term investment. Level loads require that the commission paid is spaced evenly over the time you own the fund.

Mutual funds that charge no commission to buy or sell the units are called "no-load" funds. This means there is no cost to you to buy or sell the units or transfer between funds in the same family. This also means that every dollar you invest goes to work to produce a return.

183

Commissions paid on the purchase or sale of a mutual fund can have a significant impact on the return earned on the investment. If you decided to invest $3,500 in a front-end loaded mutual fund with a commission of nine percent, of your initial investment, $315 went to pay the front-end load. Because commissions are taken directly from the amount being invested, you would really only invest $3,185 in the fund itself. That's a considerable reduction in the initial investment. If, instead, you decided to invest in a no-load fund, all your money would be used to purchase units of the mutual fund. So that additional $315 would be invested and working to meet your financial objectives.

Of course the performance of the fund itself must also be considered when choosing an investment option. Your decision should not be solely based on whether the fund has a load or not. However, it should be part of your consideration, because with even a slightly lower rate of return, the real return on a no-load fund may still be higher than on a loaded fund.

While some funds do not charge commission, they may instead charge a set-up fee. Others charge transfer fees for the privilege of transferring from one fund to another within the same group or family of funds. Finally, some mutual funds charge a termination fee to cover the administrative expense of closing an account.

MANAGEMENT FEES

All funds charge an annual management fee, sometimes referred to as an administration fee, or a management expense ratio. It pays for the administration, research and management expenses associated with the fund. This fee ranges from .5 percent to 3 percent or more a year depending on the amount of research and the types of assets held in the fund. Management fees are usually charged to the total fund and paid directly from the fund.

Management fees can have a significant impact on your return over the long term, since the higher the management fee on a fund, the more that fund must yield to produce the net return desired. For example, let's say both 123 Fund and XYZ Fund grossed 12 percent this year. The management fee on XYZ Fund is one percent, while the management fee on 123 Fund is three percent. Your net return on XYZ Fund would be 11 percent, while your net return on 123 Fund would be nine percent.

It is important that you clarify with a mutual-fund seller whether the return you're quoted is calculated before or after the management fees are taken into account. If it's after, your quoted return will reflect the net return being generated. Before you make a final decision to buy, check the return you've been quoted with an impartial source. These fees are listed in the monthly performance tables printed in major financial papers, and most returns quoted already have these fees factored in. The returns quoted in the sales pitch and in these newspapers should match.

SIMPLE RATE VS TOTAL RATE OF RETURN

Simple rate of return measures the appreciation or depreciation of the unit value of the fund over the period (typically one year, three months and year-to-date). The simple rate of return on an equity-based mutual-fund unit is calculated by dividing the capital gain/loss realized by the purchase price and multiplying by 100. If, for example, you buy an equity fund for $10 a unit and you sell it for $12, then your simple rate of return is

$$\frac{\$2 \ \text{x} \ 100}{\$10} \ = \ 20\%$$

Total rate of return measures the annual total return to investors. It includes capital appreciation or depreciation, plus interest, dividend and capital-gain distributions, which are assumed to be reinvested quarterly. The total rate of return on an equity-based mutual fund is calculated by adding together the total dividends paid and the capital appreciation (or loss), dividing it by the purchase price and multiplying it by 100. If, for example, you buy an equity fund for $10 a unit, it pays a dividend of $0.25, and you sell the unit for $12, then your total rate of return would be

$$\frac{\$2 \ + \ \$.25 \ \text{x} \ 100}{\$10} \ = \ 22.5\%$$

SOME FINAL THOUGHTS

In helping your children learn about money and build their investment portfolios, you really need to take the initiative to learn all you can about the investments you choose. The more knowledgeable you are, the more likely you will be to make the right investment decisions.

Many financial services firms offer investment seminars — often free. Take advantage of these opportunities to learn. Browse the business papers and magazines available, choose one or two that suit your needs and subscribe. Learning about investment is a continuous process. The pros have to work hard to keep abreast of what's new and different. You should also be prepared to spend a little time each week brushing up or learning new information. Learning is like life: it isn't over till it's over.

12 GOING INTO DEBT

There are almost as many reasons for borrowing as there are people, and borrowing is usually the answer when you simply don't have the money available to do what needs to be done. People borrow for things like cars, clothes, furniture and family vacations. When you take out a mortgage, you are borrowing to finance a home purchase. When you charge a sweater, book or new sofa to your credit card, you are borrowing to finance the purchase of that item. And when you write a cheque for an amount you don't have in your account and have to use overdraft protection, you're borrowing. People don't often think of things like overdraft protection and credit-card transactions as borrowing, but they are, and when there are balances outstanding they pay hefty rates of interest.

Our own attitudes about borrowing leave a strong impression on our children. My mother hated the idea of debt and she raised a daughter who looks at debt very suspiciously. Every time I have to pay a cent in interest, the hair on the back of my neck stands up. My aversion hasn't stopped me from borrowing, but it certainly has made me weigh my reasons carefully before I sign on the dotted line.

The word "credit" comes from the latin *credo* ("I believe"), and the only way you can borrow money is if someone believes you will repay that money. Borrowing is serious business. Since you're using someone else's money to buy the things you want, you have to be very aware of the fact that the lender will want his or her money back. So Golden Rule #1 of borrowing is:

If you think there's a chance you won't be able
to repay a loan, you shouldn't borrow.

DISCUSSION POINTS
What is an IOU?
What might happen if you borrowed money and then couldn't repay it?

187

Borrowing involves a promise to return the money, usually with interest. (Remember, you're renting someone else's money.) The interest calculation works in the same way it does for money on deposit, except that lenders usually charge more interest than you can earn on money on deposit. If you look back at chapter 7, you'll remember that the difference, called the "spread," is how lenders make a profit. Lenders expect to be repaid a specific amount each month, and that repayment amount includes a part of the principal — the original amount you borrowed — as well as the interest.

The higher the interest charged, the more it costs you to borrow. For example, if you decide to borrow $1,000 to get a really cool stereo system, and you're paying 10 percent in interest and repay the loan in one year, it will cost you about $100 more for that stereo. If interest rates are 12 percent, it'll cost you $120 more for the stereo. Since the higher the rate of interest, the more the item ends up costing you, Golden Rule #2 of borrowing is:

Avoid borrowing during periods of high interest rates.

Just as the rate of interest charged affects the overall cost of your purchase, so, too, does the amount of time over which you're borrowing. The longer you use someone else's money, the longer you have to pay interest, so the more you'll have to pay overall. People sometimes choose longer repayment terms so that they have lower monthly payments, which they can easily work into their spending plans. While it's a good idea not to make a promise to repay an amount you may not be able to handle, it's also important to realize that those lower payments have a cost — more interest.

MONEY LESSON
(AGE 13+)

Learning about what it costs to borrow involves comparing the cost of items bought on credit at different interest rates. Ask your child to choose an item he considers to be very expensive, such as a car, a boat or a piano, and determine what the price is for that item.

Pretend you have to borrow the money to buy that item. But before you do, you want to see what the item will actually end up costing when you include the price of using someone else's money.

If your child is old enough, let him do the calculations. If not, do the calculations with him, explaining each step so he develops an understanding of how interest is charged.

For example, if an item costs $10,000 and the rate of interest is 12 percent, the interest for one year would be $1,200:

$$(\$10,000 \times 12) \div 100 = \$1,200$$

Calculate:

- the interest cost if the interest rate was ten percent and you were borrowing the money for one year.

- the interest cost if the interest rate was 15 percent and you were borrowing for one year.

As you make your loan payments each month, a portion of your payment will be applied to the interest you owe, and the remainder will go to pay off a part of the principal. Since every payment pays off a portion of the principal, the next month's interest is calculated on a smaller amount. This is referred to as paying interest on a declining balance.

To understand how this works, you have to look at the principal (i.e., the amount you borrowed) and the interest (the cost of the loan) as two separate payments.

For example, if you borrow $5,000 at 10 percent on January 1 and your payments are $400 a month, this is how your monthly payments would be applied:

	Outstanding Balance	Monthly Interest	Monthly Payment	Applied to Principal	Principal Balance
February 1	$5,000.00	$41.66	$400.00	$358.34	$4,641.66
March 1	4,641.66	38.68	400.00	361.32	4,280.34
April 1	4,280.34	35.66	400.00	364.34	3,916.00
May 1	3,916.00	32.63	400.00	367.37	3,548.63
June 1	3,548.63	29.57	400.00	370.43	3,178.20
July 1	3,178.20	26.48	400.00	373.52	2,804.68
August	2,804.68	23.37	400.00	376.63	2,428.65
September 1	2,428.65	20.23	400.00	379.77	2,048.88
October 1	2,048.88	17.07	400.00	382.93	1,665.95
November 1	1,665.95	13.88	400.00	386.12	1,279.83
December 1	1,279.83	10.66	400.00	389.34	890.49
January 1	890.49	7.42	400.00	392.58	497.91
February 1	497.91	4.14	400.00	395.86	102.05
March 1	102.05	0.85	101.20	101.20	0.00

As you can see, since your principal goes down each month, the amount of interest you pay also goes down. Therefore more of your payment goes to paying off the principal.

Here's a simple way you can explain this concept to a child.

Molly, let's say you borrowed $1,000 and each month you repaid $200 in principal. At the beginning of the first month, you owe $1,000, so interest is calculated on the full $1,000. When you make your first payment, you will pay off $200, so now you only owe $800, and your next interest payment will be calculated on $800. When you make your next payment, you'll pay off another $200, so you will only owe $600, and so on. Because your principal is always declining, the amount of interest you have to pay keeps going down, too.

Now the calculations get really complicated, right? Luckily, financial institutions have nifty software programs that can quickly calculate the interest on a declining balance. And to keep things really simple, they do those calculations from the start so that they can give you a single payment amount that won't change over the life of the loan. This amount will repay both the principal and interest for the time frame you've selected.

MONEY LESSON

(AGE 13+)

Here's an exercise that will help to demonstrate the concept of interest on a declining balance and show how the length of the loan affects the overall amount that must be paid.

For the sake of ease, you can do this calculation as if payments were being made once a year. If you want to go into more detail, by all means do the calculations as if payments were being made once a month.

In the last money lesson, you calculated the interest on an item at 10 percent and at 15 percent for a one-year loan. Using the same item, calculate the interest, but this time use a two-year and a four-year loan period.

For example, if an item costs $10,000 and the rate of interest is 12 percent, the interest for one year would be $1,200. Since you want to repay the loan in two years, you would have to repay $5,000 a year against the principal. So at the end of the first year, you will have paid $6,200 ($5,000 in principal and $1,200 in interest).

Since you've repaid $5,000 in principal, you only owe $5,000, and that's the amount the second year's interest will be calculated on. So in the second year you would pay $600 in interest. As you can see, because you've repaid a large chunk of the money you borrowed, you'll have to pay less interest in the second year. Of course, you still have to repay the $5,000 you still owe, so in the second year you would pay $5,600 in total ($5,000 in principal and $600 in interest).

Remember to show your child how the overall cost of the item has gone up because the loan was taken for a longer period of time.

For example, if you look at how much interest you paid on a one-year loan, you can see it was only $1,200. But because you repaid it over two years — because you rented the money for a longer period of time — you had to pay more in interest. So, if you had saved up to buy the item, it would have cost $10,000. If you had borrowed and paid your loan off in one year, that item would end up costing you $11,200. And if you borrow for two years, the loan would end up costing you $11,800.

Now, let's suppose you decided to buy a second-hand car for $3,000 and your payments were $100 a month for three years. Suppose that in the second year your engine blew and it would cost much too much to have it repaired. What about the outstanding loan? Could you simply forget it?

Unfortunately, no. Even though you no longer have the use of the item you borrowed for, you are still obliged to repay the loan. So you would end up paying $100 a month for absolutely nothing. This brings us to Golden Rule #3:

When the thing you want to buy disappears before you've paid it off, the only thing you have left is the obligation to repay the debt.

MOM, CAN I BORROW...

Are you an easy touch? How many times have you *lent* your child money over the past year? How many times has your child repaid those loans?

Most of us don't think about the impressions we're giving when we cheerfully satisfy our children's desires by lending a dollar here and a dollar there. But when kids borrow regularly, they develop a habit that may last a lifetime. Should you lend money to your child? Sure. It's all a matter of laying down the ground rules and setting realistic expectations so your child learns the important lessons — the Golden Rules — of borrowing.

CAN ANYONE BORROW MONEY?

Banks won't lend their money to just anyone. First they want to be sure that the person can repay both the principal and the interest on that loan. So, lenders look at a number of things to see how likely it is that you will live up to your end of the bargain.

The first thing they try to find out about is your character. Since people usually run pretty true to form, if you've borrowed money before and repaid it on time, this is a good indication that you will do the same again. Lenders check the reference you have to give them and when they do so, they hear such character-related comments as "Oh, she's really honest" and "He always pays right on time." When they look for indications of your character, they also look at how much other debt you're carrying and if you borrow for what they consider the right reasons. They look at such things as how long you've been working and how stable your work history is, as well as how you manage your money.

The second thing they look at is your capacity or your ability to repay the loan based on the amount of money you make. If they don't think you'll be able to meet your commitments regularly, they won't lend to you. Perhaps you already have too much debt, and adding more would mean someone wouldn't get paid. Or perhaps you're job stability is in question. No job, no repayment.

The third thing they look at is your credit history. This gives them a snapshot of how you handled credit in the past. They do this by checking with a place called the credit bureau, which has a record of all your credit transactions.

Next they look at your capital, which shows how much you're worth financially. If you have lots of assets (things you own), and little debt (things you owe), then you are usually a better credit risk.

Finally, a lender will look to see if you have any collateral, which can be used to secure the loan. Collateral is an asset that can be used to help ensure the loan will be repaid. For example, if you buy a new car, the lender will likely want to use the car as collateral. If you do not repay the loan, the lender has the right to take the car and sell it to get at least some, if not all, of the loan amount back.

Most people don't understand why they are approved or declined for a loan. If they are approved, they are thankful. If they are declined, they are angry and frustrated. With a better understanding of how the process works, you can pretty well guess whether or not you will get the loan.

Understanding the things that influence lenders helps you to develop the right reputation so that you will be considered a good credit risk. Knowing, for example, that dealing in an honest and straightforward way will indicate good character, you might think twice if you are ever tempted to take a shortcut. Similarly, if you know that having too much debt may mean you are turned down for a loan when you really need it most, you might think twice about borrowing for that new toy. And if you know that by having assets that you can use as collateral you can increase your chances of getting a loan should you need one, you might work a little harder at building up those assets.

All these lessons are important for children to learn. A child who does not repay a loan on time needs to see the consequence of developing a bad credit history — no more loans. A kid who spends every cent she gets on consumable items so she has little to show for her money may need a short lesson on collateral. "Molly, if you had something you could use as collateral, we might be able to swing this loan." And the child who is constantly borrowing, may benefit from having a loan request declined to teach the importance of capacity and how constant borrowing reduces her ability to repay (and therefore qualify for) yet another loan.

If you're not sure you want to go through these types of exercises with your kids, think about how you felt the first time you had to borrow money. My knees literally shook. And my palms were so sweaty I had toilet paper rolled up in my pockets so I could dry them discreetly.

Borrowing money shouldn't put your heart in your throat. And repaying it shouldn't be an enormous burden. Credit, like all other financial instruments, is a tool. Play it correctly and you can have what you need. Learning how to use it takes time and practice. Remember, you are your child's best guide. Teach by example, but make sure the example you set is the one you want your kids to emulate.

CREDIT CARDS

A credit card such as VISA or MasterCard offers you what financial people call a "line of credit." This is a preset amount of money that you can borrow at any time and for any purpose. When you see something you want to buy, you can charge the item to the card. The bank will pay the shopkeeper, and you'll be expected to repay the bank.

Some people don't even think of using a credit card as borrowing. After all, there's no long approval process each time you want to charge something. You just charge it — *cachunk, cachunk.*

If you do not repay the full amount you have charged each month, the bank charges you interest on the outstanding balance. The interest rates on credit card are usually much higher than on other forms of credit, so carrying a balance makes using your credit card the most expensive way to pay for the things you've bought. If you are smart and pay your balance off every month on time, the bank doesn't charge you any interest at all, so you have, in effect, borrowed the money without interest for that period of time. Free money!

MONEY LESSON
(AGE 10+)

The most difficult part of learning to use a credit card wisely is developing the discipline to spend only what you can afford. This long-term lesson can be taught by issuing your own credit card to your kids.

Have your child design his own credit card. To make the card valid, you need to draw up a cardholder's agreement that both you and he will sign. This agreement should clearly state how much credit he can use, when the statement will arrive, and how much time can pass before the statement must be paid — called the grace period. It should also state the minimum

---

CARDHOLDER'S AGREEMENT

Charges can be made to this card up to a preset credit limit of $50.

Statements will arrive on the 15th of each month and you will have a grace period of 15 days, so payments must be made by the 30th of each month. The minimum payment required is 25% of the outstanding balance. If the card it not paid in full, interest will be charged on the entire balance outstanding at a rate of 24% a year, or 2% a month.

Mrs. G. McGoo

Malcolm McGoo

---

payment required and how much interest has to be paid if the balance isn't paid off on time.

Now that your child has his own credit card, he can use it when you go shopping. If he sees something he wants to buy, he will give you his card, and you'll make the purchase for him (using your card or cash). Give him a charge slip (a receipt book will work nicely) to sign, and return his card along with a copy of the charge slip.

Often when people charge more than they can afford to repay, it's a result of not keeping track of how much they've spent on their cards. As part of this exercise, have your child keep a record of how much he has spent on his credit card each month so he can anticipate how much he will have to pay at the end of the month.

If he charges more than he can pay for, or cannot make his payments on time, you, as the card issuer, have to right to cut off his credit. Once he has repaid his loan, he can start charging again. In the meantime, don't buy him stuff when you go shopping. If you do, the message you'll be sending is that he doesn't have to pay off his debts — he can just hit you up for stuff!

INSTALMENT LOANS

An instalment loan is the typical loan you take out to finance such major purchases as a car, appliances or a new roof. It is a loan of a fixed amount that requires regular payments — usually set up as a blend of principal and interest — and designed to repay the loan in total by the end of the term.

After credit cards, instalment loans are the ones most often used to finance purchases we can't immediately afford. And because they are easy to understand, they are the types of loans you can use when your kids want to borrow money.

MONEY LESSON
(AGE 13+)

The next time your child hits you up for a loan, turn it into a lesson. Use the same lending criteria that a bank would use, and set up specific repayment terms. Draw up a loan agreement and have your child sign it. Make sure the repayment terms are clearly spelled out.

If your child has borrowed before and has been inconsistent in repaying the loan, point out how this affects both her "character" and her "credit history." Tell her that before you will give her the loan, she must offer you some form of collateral. It may be her bike, her telephone or her stereo. Include a paragraph in your loan agreement that clearly spells out that if the loan is not repaid on time, you have the right to take whatever collateral she has given you until the loan is repaid.

If you child has a good credit history and you consider her a good risk, you can reward her by lowering the amount of interest you charge for the loan. Yes, you have to charge interest! And you have to charge enough interest to make the lesson worthwhile. After all, a loan at five percent on a $100 paid off in two months will only cost your kid about 80 cents — hardly enough to bring home the point.

If she defaults on the loan, you'll have to explain that you will no longer lend her money because she is not a good credit risk. Of course, in order for her to learn how to use credit, she will need a second and maybe even a third chance. So you'll have to position your decline carefully. One way to do this is to tell her that she cannot borrow money for a specific period of time — let's say three months. At the end of that period, she may apply for a loan, but she'll have to use collateral to secure her loan.

If your child consistently slips off the repayment path, you may decide to withhold a part of her allowance and apply that to the repayment of the loan. Before you take this step, think of the message you are sending by removing the responsibility for making the repayment from your child. A better lesson would be to insist upon repayment as soon as you have given your child her allowance. Create a chart showing how much she owes, and each week, reduce the amount owed so she can see her progress in repaying the loan.

A final point to remember is that if your child doesn't have the "capacity" to repay the loan, there's no positive lesson to be learned allowing her to borrow. She will default and you'll have a mess on your hands. So before you lend, make sure you are both clear on how she will repay the loan. And remember, too, that kids have a different concept of time, so a long-term loan may not be a good idea. After six months of repaying the loan, your child may feel buried and give up. Lend small amounts for short periods to start and make the repayment schedule a weekly one.

MORTGAGES

Most people don't have the money to just go out and buy a house. They have to borrow at least a portion of the money they need. Let's say, for example, that you see a house you want to buy, and it costs $80,000. That's a lot of money. Suppose you have only $20,000 saved. Well, you would use your $20,000 as a down payment and borrow the remaining $60,000. To secure the loan, the lender takes the house as collateral. In other words, if you don't repay the loan, the lender has the right to take the house and sell it to get his money back. The terms of this loan are all written down, signed and registered, and that piece of paper is called a mortgage. So, a mortgage is a loan that uses a property, such as a house or condominium, as security to ensure the debt is repaid. The borrower is referred to as the mortgagor, the lender as the mortgagee.

You can use a mortgage for financing lots of things, including purchasing a home, financing a renovation, consolidating debts and acquiring other assets. Since a mortgage is a fully secured form of financing, there's little risk to the lender. That means you usually pay a lot less interest than with most other types of loans.

The amount you can qualify to borrow is based on the amount of equity in the home. Equity is the difference between what the home is worth and any outstanding debts. For example, if the house is worth $100,000 and you put $20,000 down and take a mortgage for the rest, you have $20,000 in equity.

You can take out a mortgage on your home at any time providing you have enough equity built up. For example, if a house is worth $100,000 and you owe $60,000 on the mortgage, you have $40,000 in equity. Lenders will let you borrow against the equity in the home, so you can have use of a portion of that money for other purposes, such as investing.

Since mortgages are usually for very large amounts of money, it usually takes a long time to repay the loan. The number of years it will take to repay the entire amount of the mortgage based on a set of fixed payments is called the "amortization." For example, if a $100,000 mortgage is amortized at 10 percent over 10 years, the monthly payments would be $1,310.34. For the same mortgage amortized over 25 years, the monthly payments would be only $894.49. As you can see, the longer the amortization, the smaller the monthly payment, but the more interest paid over the life of the mortgage. Some people choose a long amortization to lower their monthly payments to meet their cash-flow needs. Others choose a short amortization schedule to reduce the amount of interest they have to pay.

MONEY LESSON
(AGE 14+)

This exercise will help to demonstrate the concept of interest on a mortgage and show how the length of the amortization affects the overall amount that must be paid. To do this exercise you'll need to buy a book of mortgage amortization tables.

Look through the real estate ads and have your child choose a home she likes. Write down the price of the house. Now, assume you have a down payment of 25 percent of the cost of the house, but need to borrow the rest. Have your child calculate:

- how much she needs to borrow

- how much her payments would be for a mortgage at 5 percent with a 10-year amortization and what her total interest cost would be

- how much her payments would be for a mortgage at 5 percent with a 20-year amortization and what her total interest cost would be

- how much her payments would be for a mortgage at 8 percent with a 10-year amortization and what her total interest cost would be

- how much her payments would be for a mortgage at 8 percent with a 20-year amortization and what her total interest cost would be

TO BORROW OR NOT TO BORROW...

Many people fear getting into debt because of their upbringing or personal beliefs. The fact is, using credit is a part of life. Whether you are financing the purchase of new appliances, replacing your furnace or financing your children's education, borrowing can offer real benefits. After all, it'd be pretty tough on the family to have to wait out a winter while you saved all the money you needed to buy a new furnace. Borrowing money, putting in the furnace and paying off the loan in easily manageable payments makes a lot more sense.

The question shouldn't simply be whether or not to borrow. Sometimes we have to. In helping your children develop good credit habits, you need to guide them in deciding when it's appropriate to borrow. Each time your child wants to borrow, help her to answer the following questions:

- Do I really need it?
- What's this going to cost me?
- What do I have to give up to buy this?

The first question relates back to the whole discussion on what a need is. Is it a want, a concern, a problem or a desire? Based on the priority of the need, you can then move to the next question.

The cost of borrowing can vary significantly, since the higher the interest rate, the greater the cost, and the longer the term of the loan, the greater the cost. Before deciding whether borrowing is appropriate, you would be wise to calculate what the item will end up costing once you've added the interest charges. Is it still worth it? Now think about how long it will take to repay the loan. Will you still be using the item? Do you still want to borrow?

The last question relates directly to the lessons in relative value. The bigger the bite the loan payments take from your cash flow, the greater the cost in terms of stress and having to go without other things. You may choose to make higher payments over a shorter term, but then you'll have to be sure your other important living needs can still be met. Kids will probably need help learning to resist the urge to steal from Peter to pay Paul. Paying off a loan quickly won't do you any good if you run up your charge cards or borrow from someone else during the process. If you choose to take a slightly longer term so that your payments are lower and fit more comfortably into your spending plan, remember this will mean a longer commitment and more interest over the full term of the loan. Help your child to weigh the answers to each of these questions carefully in deciding how she'll manage her credit needs.

10 TIPS FOR USING CREDIT

1. If you aren't sure the usefulness of a purchase will outlast the repayment period, don't borrow. It's bad enough when we spend cash on impulsive purchases, but when we have to pay for those impulsive actions way beyond the item's life, it's really hard to take.

2. If you think an instalment plan makes the deal too good to pass up, think again. That's not the right place to start. Begin by deciding whether you need the item at all, and then calculate how much you'll actually be paying in interest.

3. Adding more debt to your already high debt load is dangerous. It can lead you to the point where all or most of your income is spent on loan payments. Avoid this scenario by setting priorities before borrowing.

4. If you haven't told anyone you intend to borrow, maybe it's because you know you won't be able to justify the decision to them. Perhaps you'd like to reconsider?

5. Lots of people go shopping to cheer themselves up. Unfortunately shopping, like drinking, can cause a hangover. Ask yourself whether you'll actually feel better when the bill comes in. Adjust your perspective. Maybe a smaller, less-expensive treat will make you feel just as good. Some people need to keep up an image of success. Others shop together to build or strengthen their relationships — a smart little girl I know refers to it humorously as "female bonding." But when it comes to paying off the card or repaying the loan, it isn't so funny. Ask yourself if it's really worth it simply to impress someone else.

6. Sometimes it's easy to forget you have to pay for what you buy, particularly when you use credit cards for the majority of your purchases. If you want to stay in control of your finances and use credit wisely, stick to your spending plan and only use credit when you can easily work it into your plan.

7. Avoid impulse shopping. If you had to use cash to buy the item, would you still buy it? Will you still want it tomorrow? Next week? Next month? Next year?

8. Comparison shop for both the items you're buying and the financing you're using. Never buy anything without comparing costs and value.

9. Always read and understand any financing arrangements you are signing, particularly store financing arrangements. Understand how much the financing will cost, any fees attached and any penalties you'll have to pay. Know how much interest you'll be paying in dollars.

10. Keep track of all your credit purchases. Save your receipts or keep a written record of credit-card purchases so you can compare them with your statement. Never just pay the statement off without checking it carefully. Mistakes can be made and you may be double-charged, or charged for items you did not purchase.

THE END...
THE BEGINNING

Well, I'm done. Now, it's up to you to decide what information you'll use with your kids and how you'll begin guiding them through the money maze.

Having come all the way to the end of the book, you may have learned a bit yourself. If you have, go back and highlight some of the things you learned so that when you go through the process with your kids, you can show them that learning is a continuous process, and that you can learn right along with them.

While I've focused on the basics of money in this book, you'll likely have noticed I haven't bothered to delve into things like taxes, insurance, retirement accounts or estate planning. These are all issues that are more applicable to adults than to children. Yes, I know everyone has to pay taxes, but for the most part there isn't a lot you can do about it until you get to the stage where you can implement strategies to minimize what you pay in taxes.

There's still a lot more you can teach your children about money. Involving them in some of your financial decisions will help them relate what they are learning to the big life issues. And remember, children learn by example. So while you go about dealing with your day-to-day financial issues, don't forget that your children are watching, that the world is a wonderful place for your children to learn, and that whether you are consciously teaching them or not, they are learning.

According to all the experts, kids learn best when the learning begins early and when responsibility comes in steadily increasing, age-appropriate steps. For your children to develop a sound understanding of money and where it fits in their lives, they need to experience their money lessons within a real-world context. That means they need to be able to make their own choices and experience the consequence of those choices in ever-increasing doses. Externally imposed rules last as long as the external force. For learning to really take place, kids need to learn to internalize the rules by understanding why they exist. It's definitely worth the time to let kids make their own decisions, and learn from those decisions, be they positive or negative experiences. Remember, mistakes are lessons, just as achievements are great motivators for continued learning. Only by feeling some control over the entire process will your child develop a sense of ability and self-esteem.

As your children move through the various levels of understanding, keep talking to them. They need to be able to compare their experiences with yours. They need to share ideas and talk about alternatives. And they need to know that you're on their side — whatever the result of their decision — and that you'll help them muddle through.

If you let your children grow up with money, learning about what it will or will not do for them, making their own choices, and dealing with their successes and mistakes themselves, you'll be rewarded with children who know they have a piece of turf they can manage on their own. You can beam with pride as your child moves from begging for the latest craze to standing in front of the shelf, carefully considering the relative value of the purchase.

If your child's school doesn't currently have a course dealing with money as part of its curriculum, start pushing the peanut! Every child will have to deal with money, and therefore it only makes sense that we help our children learn what it is, how it can be used, and its role in our lives. And since your children will learn as much from their teachers and peers as they do from us at home, we want a consistent message to be delivered. Get involved in the development of the curriculum and share your ideas for helping kids to learn about money. And make sure the experience is both fun and practical for your children.

On a final note, I would love to hear your stories about how your children respond to your financial lessons. By sharing our stories, we can develop new tips and techniques for making the process of learning about money easier and more fun for our little ones. Please write to me care of the publisher. Your letters will be passed on to me.

Good luck, and have fun!

INDEX